ADVANCE PRAISE

If you've never surfed next to humpback whales, shared a personal moment with a Triggerfish, or had a bandana-wearing deer for a companion, John Merryfield's wonderful collection of deeply personal stories will take you there. His ocean world is a place of compassion and self-awareness, and his storytelling is vulnerable and compelling. There are fascinating reasons *why* he is a fish out of water, and you'll be delighted to learn them. And the best part is, you just might learn something about yourself in the process.

~ **David Robinson Simon**, author of *Meatonomics*

A moving, and at times heart-wrenching memoir, John Merryfield describes how surfing for him is more than a way of life. It is a form of spiritual exercise, a method of communion striving to heal the wounds of the world.

~ **Jasmin Singer**, author of *Always Too Much and Never Enough*

Fish Out of Water brings to life a kaleidoscope of watercolors that rests within a vast ocean through his unique experiences. I walked away with a greater appreciation of our ocean covered planet that we are gifted to call home.

~ **Benjamin Allen**, author of *Out of the Ashes, Healing in the Afterloss.*

John is a natural storyteller. This beautifully written memoir is a love letter to the ocean and her inhabitants—and a call for us all to live a kinder life.

~ **Mark Hawthorne**, author of *A Vegan Ethic: Embracing a Life of Compassion Toward All*

Fish Out of Water is tender meditation on ecology as an exterior as well as interior landscape. It is a moving response to how the natural world shapes us, and requires our attention and care. The book moves fluidly from richly descriptive scenes to reflections on how our experiences teach us to live our best life.

~ **June Slyvester Saraceno**, author of *Feral, North Carolina, 1965*

FISH OUT OF WATER

Writings from the Edge

FISH OUT OF WATER

Writings from the Edge

John Merryfield

Contents

Introduction

If I were called in
To construct a religion
I should make use of water
 ~ Philip Larkin

On my nightstand by my bed, I keep a collection of broken things. Driftwood. A broken shell. Fragments of tile. Things I find surfing, washed up along the wild, ragged shores of Baja, México.

These seemingly random artifacts, each serendipitously discovered with the wonder of an artist, represent pivotal moments when the ocean, once again, changed me. A white hot reminder that the vastness of the sea is as complex as the vast differences between the paths we take—the paths, which all too often, eventually bring us to our knees on the brilliant blue edge of our blue planet.

And there, at the smallest of openings in everything, between daylight and dark, bruised and battered, we somehow find each other, companions on the path. Or we find ourselves. Together again. Whole. The waves brought us to where we are. Or maybe it was something larger, but here we are. Like a collage, constantly being rearranged by life—the bright sting of salt lay the pieces of us. It's how everything ended up together across this time and place.

The ocean. She is the sustenance of the stories that have unfolded my life. She is the giver of life, the giver of story itself. She is the Sea: the water of my soul and the lifeblood of our planet. She is home to me.

I hope this series of short, true stories helps you find a deeper connection with the ocean that I love. *Soliloquy in the Waves* is a title to a poem by the renowned poet, Pablo Neruda, for whom the Sea was a source of constant conversation, knowledge, and beauty. For me, she is that and more. She is an endless source of reverie and refuge. The title of Pablo Neruda's poem perfectly captures the poetry I experience in her waves.

INTRODUCTION

The stories here are real and actually happened. I've changed the names of a few of the players and some surf locations to protect the privacy of the people and the sanctity of her locations.

What cannot be changed, however, is the voice of the eternal heartbeat of our ever-giving ocean.

Chapter 1

Whale Sounds Heal Wounds

His Monday mornings are littered with dried-up grapefruit rinds and leftover *semillas de marihuana.* "Check it out," Chris says with a sly grin. "I'm growing some plants," he continues, pointing to some small marijuana shoots behind his van in the sandy beach, barely evident. His faded blue Patagonia board shorts are missing a pocket in the back, like it's some sort of happy-go-lucky fashion trend.

Chris came into my life with a bang five years prior when he dropped in on a wave to go right, and I dropped in on the same wave to go left. Kaboom. After clearing ourselves from the yard-sale-wreckage of surfboards, surf leashes, arms, and legs, we ended up giving each other a laughing high-five. Our impromptu agreement? When we surf, to take ourselves less seriously. And just as importantly, to surf in opposite directions on the next wave that comes along.

A friendship began.

This morning, Chris called me over to the side of his VW van to show me his most unlikely and remarkable beach garden: a small patch of teeny, tiny marijuana plants, which he is accidently growing in the sand.

He tells me that he had just noticed them in the very spot where he dumps his sorted marijuana seeds when cleaning up. The rains from a couple of weeks ago must have fired them off. "Pretty cool, huh?"

Chris doesn't know I'm sober. Why would he? I've only declined his friendly offers of beer and pot a couple hundred times. I've also told him, you know, with my words, that I'm sober. But I get it. How is he supposed to remember stuff like that when he's living a rent-free dream on eight bucks a day in front of the warm Baja waves, growing marijuana out his back door? Tough life there.

I, on the other hand, am juggling my work life as a house painter in California with the life I'm building in México. I just drove a solid hour on a lonely Baja highway in a rusted skateboard—an '84 Dodge Colt, to get to the waves. I left a Monday morning construction project on my modest single-story Mexican colonial home in Buenavista to do so.

This project, which started modestly but became the most harrowing one of my life, is quickly losing its charm. It's time-consuming, money draining, and quickly turning me into a stressed-out curmudgeon.

To top it off, not having access to the escape of weed or alcohol to take the edge off makes it that much more challenging. That's a luxury I lost, or never quite had to begin with. Bequeathed the alcoholic gene, I realized that there are some people who can drink and some people who shouldn't drink. I am the latter. And besides, I have a wife now, even grandkids to consider—the whole beautiful catastrophe of life. As appealing at it sometimes is, unlike Chris, I don't have time to grow a miniature marijuana farm.

I can hear the rhapsody of the ocean, and I'm eager to surf. I pitched the shovel and tools this morning, abandoning the remodel project at my house, and grabbed my surfboard. I've been working too much on the house, adding on a small bedroom and closing off walls and ceilings to the oftentimes squalls of weather and invading armies of insects. Prior to the remodel, the house was no more than a Palapa shade structure, open to those dastardly cucarachas. I needed a break—a surf break (as if there's any other kind?).

But when I look at Chris, the irony is not lost on me. He barely works. He lives on the beach. He pays no rent. He surfs every day. He leisurely reads books under the shade of a nearby coconut palm tree. And unlike me, he can drink a beer once in a while, and smoke some pot without the relentless pull for more. The last time I visited, I actually saw him drink half a beer and leave the rest. What a waste! I admit it. I thought of that half-a-beer well into the night, long after leaving (I don't call myself an addict for nothing). And to top it off, like Johnny-Marijuana-Appleseed, he has such a lucky touch with growing dope, that he simply throws the seeds on the beach and watches them grow—no nurturing required. It's just too much sometimes.

Why would I collapse my vision to land head-on a single person like Chris? The reason is because he's a colorful kaleidoscope for my surf envy to focus on. Chris represents freedom and ease—and ecstasy—with waves, old surfboards, and drugs and alcohol.

I've only had a few times in my now 30-year sobriety where I've been stopped in my tracks by my baffling and bankrupt thoughts. This is one of them. This is one of those times when I'm not good enough, not free enough, not happy enough, not whole enough. I feel like a bird's nest in December. Empty.

Ok, maybe it's been more than just a few times I've felt this way. Come to think of it, perhaps many, many times. The last time was at a friend's house-warming party in a neighborhood called, of all things, Looney Loop. Much like today, on that day, I was happily sober (sober and happy; it's an oxymoron), and I was staring at a fancy tray of lovely red, yellow, and green tequila Jell-O shots as they went jiggling across the room. I think, wow, my life could be so much better! The alcoholic in me says sobriety is for the uninspired. But Jell-O shooters, now that's living! You see? It's tricky.

There's no rhyme or reason to it. No logic. All it took is for Chris to show me the results of his *green thumb,* and bingo: Instant insanity. How could such a lack of proportion, and the ability to think straight, be characterized any other way than insane?

This addict-demon of mine is a familial one. Its depth and breadth can be triggered by the ordinary, or by the extraordinary. A reservoir of melancholy can arise from those endless choppy waters until I'm there, floating alone, separate from others—split away from the source of goodness—my insecurity, doubt, and despair whispering a monologue of untruths.

Being happy for Chris and his endless-summer lifestyle seems like a more reasoned reaction. And what the hell is so bad about my life? I chuckle at my childish petulance. I live half the year in beautiful Lake Tahoe where I work, and I live the other half of the year with my wife in Baja, where we write poetry, eat mangos, and surf. All of which, by the way, would be a distant murmur, a phantom parallel life, if not for sobriety.

Sobriety is the lifeline connecting me to my true self, my oceanic self.

But I want more. More life. More beauty. More love. More joy. More poetry. Apparently, the missing piece in my life is a teeny, tiny marijuana grove growing free and wild on the beach for me to admire before going surfing. Now that's living.

Chris's life isn't absent of problems. He can't seem to find a steady girlfriend to share his hobo surf dream. Despite his aloof, surfer dude exterior, I know that it pains him to not have someone to share his life with. He can't seem to find a girlfriend to share his charmingly vagabond's slice of paradise, and not for lack of trying. Chris admits to it being a tough sell with the ladies; they don't seem to appreciate the freedom and simplicity we do. Nope. Those rascals see the hardships, the instability, and the lack of pillows and a functioning toilet.

By the time Chris paddles out to the waves, I've already caught a few waves and the surf has washed off most of my angst. With only Chris and me in the water, there are plenty of waves to ride.

The two of us are sitting on our surfboards with our legs dangling in the ocean at a surf spot called Shipwrecks, on the East Cape of the Baja Peninsula. A simple little swell is pumping up from the Southern Hemisphere. Feeling the medicinal energy of the waves, I am amazed yet again at how the edges of my broken pieces are so easily smoothed by the polished sea. By how quickly I am returned to wholeness—a fragile equilibrium. I feel like Duke Kahanamoku when he said, "Out of the water, I am nothing."

Yet in the ocean, I am an aggregate of all that is real. I am free of identity—a nonentity in human terms, just the way I like it. The spindrift energy of the waves frees me from myself. I am one among many: the dolphins, whales, a yellow reef fish, a bloated puffer fish, a squadron of brown pelicans … even the *agua-malas* with their stinging ways lets me know I'm alive. I'm a part of something bigger.

Saltwater is the thread of our connection.

Several head-high waves go unridden as Chris and I scramble over the first wave of the set of three to position ourselves for the larger, cleaner waves to follow. This addictive anticipation is part of the reason I show up for the waves; every single time, they show up for me, too.

And just like that, too lost in the dreamy rhythms of surfing to notice the kind of sight that surfer's text their friends about to make them jealous. A female Humpback whale and her one-year-old baby are tail-slapping the water a hundred short yards from us. I look back toward shore to see a Mexican man with his left hand on top of his head in amazement and his right hand pointing out to the whale. He's yelling, or singing, or whistling. I'm not sure which. The man is making the happy kind of sounds you would hear in Mexican Banda music.

For ten minutes, the whales are upside-down to our world of complexities announcing their significance: thawp, thawp, thawp. These magical beings provide an alternative to the Mexican adage, *"Vale mas un grito a tiempo que hablar a cada momento,"* which translates to, "Better one timely squawk than a constant talk."

I can hear the constant drumbeat of sound through the rumble of the waves as I surf. I am reminded of the late poet Mary Oliver's instructions for living the life of a poet, "Pay attention. Be amazed. Tell about it." The Humpback whales' commanding tail slaps seem to say, "Life is wonderful! Listen to this!" And so I do.

As if following Mary Oliver's poet instructions to the T, I slide off my surfboard into her warm waters to investigate the possibility of hearing the whale sounds below the surface—and I can. The distant moaning and muffled pops from the tail slaps underwater pass through the outer walls of the wounded, broken part of myself. They pass through the space within me that becomes unglued with fear or greed. They pass through the addict in me that wants to romance the dreamy, colorful tequila Jell-O shots as they float by on trays of delight—as I once had done, before life had slapped me in the face and told me to stop.

These impeccable sounds pass through the remnants of despair and the subtle layers of ego. At this moment in time, I begin and end here, under this wave, where everything is possible and regret knows nothing of me.

The tail slaps and eerie moaning of the great Humpback whale song underwater hit me directly in the chest. The whales share an ancestral and lonesome communication, with surprising moments of playfulness.

The anguish and beauty are startling. My mind is transported, as if struck by the mallet of a singing bowl. The healing for the day is complete. Momentarily returning me to wholeness, I have no wants, no desires. There's no wish to escape. There exists no drug as large, no drug as powerful as this reality. I have no desire to be anyone other than me, to be anywhere other than here. I simply have now.

Complicit No More

For 50 million years, the Humpback and Gray whales have migrated 6,000 miles along the western coast of North America from their summer feeding grounds in the icy, fertile waters of the Bering Sea to their winter birthing lagoons and playgrounds here in Baja, México. Twice they've been hunted to the brink of extinction.

Douglas Adams, no stranger to irony, wrote, "On the planet Earth, man had always assumed that he was more intelligent than dolphins because he had achieved so much—the wheel, New York, wars, and so on—whilst all the dolphins had ever done was muck about in the water having a good time."

It's difficult to imagine how or why more than 120 pregnant whales were killed recently along with 213 other whales during a hunt off the coast of Antarctica. To have such little compassion is astonishing. Japan seems determined to live in the Dark Ages by continuing to kill and consume these awe-inspiring animals, including pregnant females.

And all of us who continue to eat fish are complicit in allowing over 650,000 marine animals, including whales, dolphins, seals and turtles to be *accidently* killed in fishing nets each year.

But there is nothing accidental about it. Routinely, this kind of bloodshed occurs year after year. With numbers like those, killing whales and other marine life is a part of doing business; it's just baked into the product. Dead whales in fishing nets are just as much a part of the fish-fillet sandwiches I used to enjoy as are the dead whales of Japan's whale hunts.

Just as the ocean moves me, so do its inhabitants. They inspire me with their unapologetic authenticity. Of course, it wasn't always this way. I can remember not too long ago when my life looked very different, hidden by societal norms and expectations. It was during those days that I did what I feel now is unthinkable: I too was complicit in the death of more than 650,000 marine animals, including whales, dolphins, seals, and turtles.

How does surfing succeed to elevate my consciousness where religion or conventional spiritual-practice falls short? The reason is because the ocean places me directly in the path of wonder, connecting me to the world around me in a deep and profoundly personal way. We may be hard-wired for this connection with the ocean; indeed, we came from water. I'm not referring to our time spent drifting as a single cell organism in the primordial oceanic soup. I'm referring to our more recent home of origin: the womb.

The amniotic fluid is 99 percent the same as seawater, so the ocean is our original home. Water is our original medicine. She aids in our wellbeing, and even provides feelings of transcendence. There's science behind how the simple observation of water changes us. Even when we just think of a stream, a fountain, a Koi fishpond, tropical reef fish in the ocean, a warm bath, swimming, surfing, we are brought to depths of relaxation and calmness. It is not a coincidence.

Our blood is 80 percent water content, although my blood may be closer to 100 percent. According to my mother, when I was a baby, no more than 1ten months old, I was already swimming underwater, doing laps across the pool with little baby breaststrokes. My parents were amazed the first time my father set me in water to feel the buoyancy of the swimming pool. I started swimming circles around him, head down holding my breath, head up for a lungful. I could swim before I could walk. A fish was born.

The watery portion of our blood, the plasma, has a concentration of salt and other ions, which are remarkably similar to seawater. We desire a deeper connection with the ocean. We need a deeper connection to her.

We are each mini-oceans—wild, robust, salt-water seas. Rumi, the great Sufi mystic poet described it like this: "You are not a drop in the ocean. You are the entire ocean in a drop." Yet we peer out onto a sea of humanity with a separate, limited sense of self. In reality, it is the larger source from which we came. Our unity is the ocean itself and beyond.

Without her, I would not be. Without her, we would not be. Without her, our battered and brokenness would not find wholeness. Without her, our addictions would become our gradual dire alchemy. Without her, we would not come together in our wholeness ... in her wholeness.

That afternoon driving away from Shipwrecks—the surf spot, and Chris's surf camp on the edge of the Sea, with salt crystals drying on my skin, I can't help but think of my wife Carol. I'm going home to see her. She is home for me. But I'm also leaving my home—the ocean. I navigate these contrasting worlds in search of oneness.

Chapter 2

RULE #1

Koko said, "Never turn your back on the ocean. This is rule number one."

The rule is a metaphor for respect. It's about how the ocean gives us life; how she is a way of life. How she is life.

At Waikiki, it was Koko who taught me how to surf. He was an enormous Samoa-Hawaiian who had shiny round shoulders and wild black palm-tree hair that relentlessly and adamantly stuck straight up.

I was ten years old when I learned how to surf. The grade school teasing about my own hair—long, with its natural tendency to change color with the seasons—felt particularly personal at that age. My hair color would easily change tones in the sun, naturally, without colorant. When in

California in the wintertime, it would be brown. When in Hawai'i in the summertime, it was blonde. The kids called me Miss Clairol, after the women's hair coloring product. This struck close to my core, as if to say, it's not okay to be who I am.

My father had a small car rental business on Maui called the West Side U-Drive, where I worked washing cars every summer until I was fifteen. The car rental had a small fleet of about ten rusted, beat-up Datsuns. Rope and bungee cords seemed to hold some of the cars together. I learned how to drive when I was just twelve, including the more complex manual transmissions, so I could shuffle the cars around in order to wash off the red Hawaiian pineapple plantation dirt.

When I wasn't at the family business working, I was in the surf.

Until I learned how to board surf, body surfing was how I spent my time in the ocean. I spent more time in the salty waters of the Hawaiian Islands than I did on land. My face and shoulders were always burned from the sun and my eyes would sting at the end of each day from the high salinity levels of the water.

Never turn your back on the ocean.

If you're standing along the shore, or in the water surfing with your back to the waves, you can't see a wave coming. Not seeing a wave coming is a bad thing. The wave will not simply knock a person down; she will pull you out with her. And in Hawai'i, that is no small thing.

Whenever I'd be riding those gigantic waves, it was Koko who masterfully delivered those life lessons. This big Samoan would say, "You never turn your back on your family. The same goes for the ocean. She is family, so you never turn your back on her." I learned that surfing was as much about caring about the ocean as it was about catching the perfect ride.

Admittedly, the Hawaiian beachboys "safety-first" mentality was dubious at best. Since I learned how to surf so quickly, I would go out surfing on my own. Alone.

It was one especially clear August afternoon when the hot dog beachboys were coming through the surf zone in their outrigger canoes. They were skimming by very close to us surfers just to show off. But it was, in fact, too close. One of the beachboys accidently ran me over in his outrigger canoe while the two of us were trying to catch the same wave. I sustained a serious concussion.

Later, that same dude found me sitting on the beach holding my head and squinting at the waves that I was now too woozy to ride. "Oh hey, look out! You okay? You gotta look behind ya, little brah. Never turn your back! You okay? Yeah, you okay. You surfer now, brah!"

His Pidgin English emphasized the alpha-male-Hawaiian in him. To him, I was a Haole, an outsider.

Being a white person, a non-native Hawaiian in Hawai'i, has its challenges and its rewards. Feeling the Aloha-love can be overwhelmingly good with the sense of unity and welcoming spirit. On the other hand, being a Haole in the surf can feel as heavy as that irksome concussion that still, thirty years later, makes me wince.

It was a tough-love lesson about "never turning your back." Thrown in for good measure, it was also a lesson about the right-of-way rules for surfing a wave. The person behind you, or on the inside of the wave, has the right of way. This is especially true if what is behind you is a 6'4" Hawaiian with a poi belly surfing in an outrigger. Lesson learned.

The Hawaiian spirit of Aloha and ocean conservation each have strong roots in the Polynesian culture. Humans and the ocean are inextricably linked. The Polynesians knew this, and held a strong sense of stewardship, pride and spiritual connection with the sea. They relied on the sea for food, water, and transportation for survival while also utilizing the ocean for ceremony and recreation. Staying in balance with the ocean means to stay alive. To respect her waves, to respect her weather, to respect her interconnected life—the air, the fish, the plants—to respect her depths, the unseen realms that create life, is a way of life.

The Hōkūleʻa for example, made a huge impression on me when I was a kid in the 70s. The Hōkūleʻa was a replica of the Polynesian double-hulled ancient voyaging canoe. Its goal was to demonstrate using ancient "wayfinding" techniques of ocean knowledge and celestial navigation. The Hawaiians from Polynesia are a result of purposeful sailing trips through the Pacific Ocean, as opposed to passive drifting with the currents. In that sense, ocean conservation for the Hōkūleʻa was a way of life.

These ancient wayfinding techniques included the use of stars, wind and weather patterns, ocean currents and wave direction, and the flights of birds and their migration patterns. All of these methods and more meant that Island people had to know the ocean—had to be close to her, to feel the ecological balance and share in that balance. There was mythology and science to their relationship with the ocean, and the Hōkūleʻa was a resurrection of those ancient ways of life.

When the Hōkūleʻa returned to the Ala Wai harbor on Oahu from Tahiti on July 26, 1976, I was among thousands of people to greet them. Outrigger canoe paddlers and surfers were in the ocean paddling alongside the Hōkūleʻa. People standing on shore were throwing flower leis into the water. The joy, the Hawaiian pride, the ocean pride, the flowers, the Aloha spirit, were all unforgettable.

The Hōkūleʻa also showed me that even the ancient Hawaiians were also once outsiders, like Haoles. They were foreigners who traveled across the ocean to find a new home in Hawaiʻi.

To this day I'm an outsider of sorts, similarly to when I was a kid as a Haole in Hawai'i. I'm an American living in Mexico. Now I am referred to as a Gringo.

While the origin, and the use of the word Gringo may have, in the past, had a derogatory connotation, the present day usage of the word Gringo seems to simply refer to a foreigner of any kind, and nothing else. According to my Mexican friends and others I've talked to about the word Gringo, it's used to refer to folks like me without resentment, nor ill will. It's just as a matter of fact, as obvious as the ocean.

Being considered a foreigner in a foreign land is something I'm used to. The fact is there is but one sure location I've always belonged: the ocean.

The land itself is more foreign to me. I may be a Gringo, or a Haole—a fish out of water of sorts—but not while in the water. The ocean is my second home; her waters are my place of ease and comfort. In her waves, her unending waves, I am at home.

As a kid in Hawai'i, I would spend hours and hours in the
ocean. Measuring myself against the blue immensity of the
Sea. My younger brother Jim and I would surf laps around
each other. The Lahaina Harbor, and the Kahana reef on
Maui, were our local breaks. The connection of family is
deeper when shared with the ocean.

A waterman is a person who is strong and capable in the
ocean and who participates in multiple water sports. By
thirteen years old, I thought of myself as an ocean
waterman. I was a competitive swimmer, a surfer, a
bodysurfer, and a free diver.

The famous Hawaiian waterman, Duke Kahanamoku, was
one of my childhood heroes. I also admired a big-wave
Hawaiian waterman named Eddie Aiku, who valiantly died
trying to paddle fifteen miles to Moloka'i for help when his
Hōkūle'a was swamped in the open ocean. His spirit and
brave heart made an impression on me.

I listened very closely to the older Hawaiian surfers while
out on the waves. They talked about surfing like it was
religion; Outrigger canoe paddling like they were devotees.

These ocean warriors also spoke about how spearfishing can be a part of a connection to the ocean. They described it in a reverent way, with a sincere spirit and a true desire to connect with the ocean. I looked up to them and wanted to be like them. So just like that, I wanted to learn to spearfish as well.

I bought a spear gun that looked like a javelin pole with a rubber band at one end and sharp pointy spears at the other. My mom didn't want me to use the hand-held pneumatic powered spear gun that shot like a pistol. She was afraid that I might accidently shoot myself or my brother with it. As it turns out, the pole style spear is more difficult to catch fish with than is the pneumatic gun.

Becoming proficient at spearfishing was a challenge. I speared a few small fish. But truthfully, I was a little upset by the experience. The wiggling fish—the suffering at the end of my spear—pierced my own emotions. I didn't want to listen to those emotions, to the voice of sensitivity and empathy. As I stared at my spear gun, I was suddenly brought back to being a little tyke in Southern California where my dad was teaching me how to fish in the Newport Harbor. I cried when the fish I hooked came out of her home, the water at the end of my fishing line. I was so sad. The poor fish, I thought. I did that!

At just thirteen, I wanted to leave that softer self behind me. I thought I needed to relinquish the more feminine, concerned side of myself. I was just a mama's boy, I thought. Years later, it became evident to me that societal norms were banking on boys like me squelching our inherent sensitivity. This is indeed a familiar story.

So, by the time I was able to spearfish, I told myself that I needed to be emotionally stronger than when I was a kid. I needed to rise above what I considered to be my former childhood reactions about killing fish. I needed to be a man, whatever that meant.

Instead of recoiling at the thought of causing pain to a sea creature, I needed to think of fishes as offerings of the ocean. I told myself that I would be taking only what I needed, and no more. I also told myself that the fishes' suffering would be over quickly, and that their life was a gift to us.

These were not original thoughts of mine. They were, and still are, a part of an overall narrative that we carry within the culture, including the Hawaiian culture—and for that matter, in most cultures and societies of the world. We tell ourselves convenient stories: the inventions of our mealtime prayers—fish want us to eat them, and they are the primary reason the ocean exists. It is there to feed us—a gift from God.

I wanted to be a real waterman, a real man. I wanted to be like the Hawaiians, capable of all ocean activities, so I kept trying. I had also talked to some of the local restaurants, and in my exaggerated self-confidence, I had already made arrangements to provide fresh fish to them in exchange for money. I didn't want to let them down. I had to learn quickly.

The idea is simple: Dive down, hold your breath, wait motionless for a fish to swim by, and then spear it.

Moving slowly and being stationary helps you blend in with the ocean. To look as though you belong, like you've always been there—a common piece of furniture. The trick is to seem less like a human—the clumsy, awkward, herky-jerky land animals we are.

To be fluid and to appear fish-like came naturally to me. I felt like a fish. I moved in her waters like a fish would move. My legs porpoise in the water, my torso and core are strong, and I could breath-hold relatively well. I could recognize her currents without any effort, and I understand waves. I was also good at relaxing underwater and remaining still and calm.

As I progressed with my spearfishing experiment, I was diving in a cove off of the west side of Maui in about twenty feet of water.

By my third or fourth dive down, I still hadn't caught anything, but I was determined. I dove down again, holding my breath, equalizing my ears on the way down. I got to the bottom of the ocean floor, about twenty feet deep. I remained there, perfectly still. I waited.

The seconds ticked by with no fish in view, my oxygen slowing evaporating. I could see several fish in the distance, but none of them came my way. "Relax," I told myself. "The calmer I am, the less oxygen I will use. The slower my heart rate is, the longer I can stay down."

Suddenly, from behind my back, came a beautiful one-foot long Triggerfish. She had a chubby mouth and the top of her upper lip was the perfect shade of blue. Teal stripes ran across her head and yellow-orange markings down her back. She propelled herself using waving motions from her dorsal fins. She came from behind my left side, unseen, stopping directly in front of me—right in front of my face—at eye-level. My right arm outstretched, with the spear in position in front of me. But the spear was way too far forward to be useful to spear her, which is, as the kids these days would say, *all up in my grill.*

I couldn't tell if she was being friendly or aggressive. She was so close to me that it momentarily threw me. I didn't have a chance to organize myself to get a shot off. Either that, or I actually didn't want to. Her delicate fins fluttered like twin-engine helicopter blades. Her mouth was slightly open, her lips pursed. She looked as though she was trying to vocalize something. I might have even heard a faint grunt, like a pig. She looked like a real lady—slightly regal.

Instead of swimming away from me, she just hovered there, looking at my face, looking into my mask. My wide eyes must've look wild; I was stunned. She was so close that I could probably reach out and grab her.

But I didn't. I didn't want to.

We both stared motionless into each other's eyes. Even in retrospect, I can't quite make sense of it. The mutual recognition we had with each other was equal to the kind of moments I had when I would meet a person or a dog for the first time. There you are—here I am. We see each other. I mean, we really connect.

I came to the cove to kill a fish. But this magnificent Triggerfish came over to me—to make an introduction. Little did I know that this introduction was really to the rest of my life's purpose.

The moment seemed to last forever, but it was no more than ten seconds, maximum. By the time I depleted my oxygen and needed to go up, she slowly wandered away. Releasing all of the air out of my lungs, I broke the surface and I breathed again.

Instantly, everything was different. I knew who I was, and I knew who I wasn't. I also knew who the ocean was, and who she was not. That Triggerfish, and that moment long ago, have carried me in every moment since.

I had heard fishermen describe Triggerfish as ugly, poorly designed, brainless, and of little value. The magnificent creature who looked into my eyes, however, was none of these.

The Hawaiians refer to Triggerfish as humuhumunukunukuāpua'a and consider them to be a symbol of Hawai'i. The song, "My Little Grass Shack," in Kealakekua Hawai'i, includes a line: "...where the humuhumunukunukuāpua'a go swimming by...".

Well, a humuhumunukunukuāpua'a had just swum by me and I was forever changed. And I knew it, too. It didn't just change my mind; it changed my heart.

I was done spearfishing for the day. I was done spearfishing for good.

The next day, I went surfing with my buddy Bradley. We looked at the waves, measuring the height of dwarf palm trees. Bradley was an older friend of mine. I admired his surfing and I trusted him. To this day, he's one of the nicest guys I have ever known.

As we were waxing our surfboards, getting ready to go out in the waves, I described the strange encounter I'd had with a Triggerfish—how close I was physically to her, how close I felt to her. But I downplayed the heart-to-heart part of the experience. I was playing it cool; I didn't want him to think of me as a wuss.

He said, "Yep, Triggerfish can, in fact, make grunting noises. Maybe she had some un-hatched eggs. It could have been some form of aggression."

Aggression? What I had seen in the Triggerfish was a creature who was confidant, curious, and self-assured. But it is quite possible that she was protecting family. If she had un-hatched eggs to guard, or her mate nearby, the mama Triggerfish looking after her family could have been a possible scenario. Familial ties can bring out the deepest emotion, the fierceness in all of us.

This was around the time when my grandmother passed away. My thoughts too were with family. My very own family was grieving from the absence of a loved one. My grandmother died on the Jersey Shore, where my grandparents had retired. My mom went back east for the service while the rest of the family—Dad, brother, and sister—all stayed home in Hawai'i. It was a sad time. Our hearts held together by the thread of a long-distance phone line.

Bradley then joked, "Glad you're okay! Maybe next time you'll actually spear the fish!"

And once again, I was a stranger in a strange land—the land of the Haole, the land of the Gringo, the harsh, unfamiliar land on the edge of the sea.

I was quiet as we paddled out into the waves, too shy to talk about how I didn't want to kill that Triggerfish, or any other fish. At the time, I didn't know how to put into words how she had touched me.

I knew I would sooner or later have to somehow explain what happened to me and why I no longer would be spearfishing. I also knew that my restaurant friends would be expecting fish to be delivered—and would ask.

What should we call someone who cares, someone who connects with the ocean and her inhabitants? Human? How about humane? Humane is a parallel variant of the word human—having the qualities befitting of human beings. Humane means: to be compassionate, kind, sympathetic, good-natured, and gentle. I see those characteristics as inherent to being a human being. I also see those characteristics as inherent to me being me.

There are many statues in ocean countries around the world of men throwing spears into the ocean, catching fish. Those statues are made of steel and bronze. They are proud looking. Strong. There are fewer statues of Gandhi in the world—fewer statues of men holding walking staffs—practicing nonviolence.

I, too, aspired to be like Duke Kahanamoku, not Gandhi. I didn't even know who Gandhi was at the time.

At the very moment I got out of the water with the Triggerfish, I knew things were different. I also knew that it didn't matter to me what she was or was not doing in front of me that day. It doesn't matter what she was or was not communicating to me. What matters is what I felt about what I saw. And what I saw in the Triggerfish was a brave, calm, and secure individual. In her, I saw someone who knew what they were doing and someone who knew what they wanted to do. What I saw was *someone* with whom I am worthy of sharing the ocean. What I didn't see was *something* that I wanted to take from our ocean.

And what I felt was a kinship with her. I felt a connection. I felt compassion for her, although at the time I didn't know what compassion truly was. The heartfelt familial ties were as if she were a part of my clan, in my tribe, like family. I felt sympathy, humility, remorse. I felt like a small person for even holding the intention of taking her life in the first place.

The Hawaiians taught me how to appreciate and understand Mother Nature. They taught me how to read her waves. They taught me how to surf like royalty—proud, yet humble. They taught me what Aloha means: Aloha 'aina, aloha kai. It means *love the land, love the sea, and only take what you need.*

I've not eaten fish since that day. *Only take what you need.*

Fish are not just a commodity, not just pieces of meat. I see them for the individuals they are. They are not objects. Fish are social creatures, good-natured, sometimes shy, sometimes curious, sometimes aggressive. Just like me.

My affinity for the ocean is not unique. Humans come from water. We are made most mostly of water. We are born to connect with her.

The message I was telling myself at thirteen years old was constructed on a lie. I didn't need to "man-up."

A soft heart is a good thing. A soft heart is a natural thing. Compassion and empathy are normal; they are as normal and natural as the water itself.

Toughening up my heart was not, and still is not, the answer. My aquatic self, whose heart was touched by a beautiful fish, guided me in that moment, and still guides me today.

Never turn your back on the ocean.

Koko's relaxed Pidgin English instructed me: "You never turn your back on your family," he said. "The same goes for the ocean. She is family, so you never turn your back on her."

I'm glad I didn't turn my back on her that day. I'm glad I didn't turn my back on myself that day, either. Today, I could never imagine spearing a fish—someone I consider to be a friend, a family member, an ocean being, a fellow swimmer, a surfer, and a fellow earthling.

Love the land, love the sea, and only take what you need.

I want to take from the sea only what I need. And the only need I have from her is her love. She is family. She is the giver of life and I am eternally grateful for her love. That is all I wish to take. That is all I need to take. Her love.

Chapter 3

THE SHINING PATH

Punch drunk by moonbeams in the ocean, I was twenty miles from my destination—Cabo Pulmo. I'd been paddling my fourteen-foot SUP board for the last four hours in the middle of the night.

Before leaving home, Carol's note of encouragement read: *The pink geranium blossoms are marking your path back to the Sea. Follow them.* With just a few words, her poetry can transport me from uncertainty to a vision of Eden.

The Mexican desert air in January was cool and dry. Breaching Modula rays are heard but not seen, with belly flops slapping the water. Seawater soothed my feet.

At night, the ocean has an added dimension. The Milky Way and waning moon at their zenith were now also below me, reflecting off the surface of the ocean. It felt impossible to distinguish where the vastness of the ocean ended and where I began.

My paddle stroked the sparkling moonlight around me.

And yet, the smell of diesel, old fish, and cigarettes sent caution signals to my mind, reminding me that there was another world here.

I saw the bright but distant boat lights and heard their rumbling diesel motor as they crisscrossed the ocean. Commercial shrimp trawlers—two boats with working lights off their stern—rumble across her silky surface, and too near to me.

Quenching a deep thirst lemon-water from my hydration pack, I questioned my own sanity. Why paddle forty miles here in México from my house in Buenavista to Cabo Pulmo? What possibly could have pulled me deeper into the distance and further from shore?

I no longer paddled the yearly, non-stop, 72-mile SUP around Lake Tahoe. 2018 was my eleventh and final year. I thought I was finished with SUP endurance paddling.

The journeys around Lake Tahoe were to inspire people to adopt a vegan diet. As I had hoped, those who watched me paddle—both in person and through the various media outlets that covered my efforts—were turned on to the plethora of benefits veganism presents. Many were enlightened to the fact that cruelty to animals is, under any and all circumstances, egregious and unnecessary.

But I wanted to move on to other endeavors, other adventures. To surf more, write, walk on the beach, lie in the hammock as the afternoon came and went. Being landlocked behind gates of giant cardón cactus while swaying in the hammock, the sea became my dream, my escape.

Lying in the hammock feeling hopeless about the world didn't do me any good. I needed to do something. When feeling powerless and downhearted, I went to the ocean to find refuge. The sea teaches me, each and every time. The madness between my ears is pacified by the rhythm of the ocean's wide expanse, and there I feel the upwelling of hope.

I found myself daydreaming, in Baja, looking down the coast toward Lighthouse Point and beyond, wondering if I could paddle to Cabo Pulmo. Drawn to her side, to feel her motion in another dance of great distance.

So there I was on the Sea of Cortez in the middle of the night—a kook on a SUP with moonbeams in my eyes. The saying goes: *I used to suffer from insanity; now, I enjoy it.*

Cabo Pulmo is a protected national park here in México. It is a sanctuary, and one of the most important areas of the Sea of Cortez. Its importance lies in the large number of marine species, now protected from fishing. The 25,000-year-old living coral reef is one of only three remaining living reefs in North America. Marine Biologist Sylvia Earle calls it a Hope Spot—a special place that is critical to the health of the ocean, a place to give us hope. A place to show us that ocean protection works.

Protected from human exploitation since 1995, the coral reef of Cabo Pulmo transformed into an oasis of rich biodiversity. Fish biomass increased by 460 percent, bringing the reef to a level of life similar to that of pristine coral reefs that have never been fished. Keystone species like sharks, the marine ecosystem's apex predator, also made a comeback.

My pilgrimage to Cabo Pulmo is not meant for publicity. It's more personal than that. I need hope.

All of us need more hope.

Recently, on a flight from Los Angeles down to Los Cabos, I was sitting in the aisle seat next to a young girl and her mother. Just after takeoff, the girl announced to her mother, "I can see the entire world!" Her face was alive with wonder. Instantly, I fell in love with her high-pitched little voice. "The entire world, Mom! Look! It's everywhere!"

The young girl's mother was head deep in *People*. She barely lifted her head toward her daughter, eventually offering a vacuous half-smile. "My God," I thought. "The world of wonder ... shit-canned with a head tilt and a cold shoulder!"

But I looked around the airplane and realized that no one was having very much fun—nor did they even seem to have a pulse nor other vital signs. All heads bowed in trounced unison, with most of the window shades to the outside world closed shut. The collective despondency would have made more sense had we been bound for some dark, dusty coalmine for a hard day of labor—but not this; not en route to sunny Los Cabos, México. It was a bleak and hopeless crowd.

I wondered where the service dogs were when we really needed them—the ones who wear a blue vest, lick people's hands, and smell bad? Slobbering, happy-go-lucky service dogs, with their tongues hanging out and their tails wagging. At least the presence of a goofy dog could bring some life into this sad little airplane.

Many of Earth's delicate ecological systems seem to be on the brink, and we, in fragile flight, don't seem to care enough about our little aircraft; Planet Earth has entered into a graveyard spiral. Even the most ardent deniers have heard the forecasts, and deep down inside—in the less defiant part of themselves—they know the truth.

Humanity seems to be heading toward calamity with the window shades closed and our heads buried deep in *People* magazine.

A fishless ocean from overfishing. Species extinction. Ocean warming. More plastic than ocean life. Acidification. Reef bleaching. And on and on it goes.

We hear the news. We hear doom. We hear the gloom.

Sylvia Earle touts Cabo Pulmo as a *hope spot*. My mind wanders as I paddle. I'm going to where the hope is: Cabo Pulmo.

The water took me gently up and down with the short breaths of wind generating swells and yawing my SUP board. Back and forth with the Sea of Cortez swell.

Fatigue, elation, tedium, and expansiveness were available around me and within me.

At times, during my time on the water, I ruminated on the relationships in my life, the connections, and the conversations I'd had, or conversations I needed to have. I felt gratitude for all the people, all the animals, and the glorious ocean. Past endurance paddles came to my memory—the successes, the hardships, everything in between.

During the night, this part of the Sea of Cortez was calmer—with less wind and fewer waves, and the air temperature was cooler to aid paddling longer distances.

The night wasn't without challenges. Thrashing sounds in the water from small fish avoiding my path became bogeymen in the dark. They were most likely the sounds from a roosterfish or a Dorado, but in the blackness, my mind imagined them to be a huge shark. Also, when the fin of my SUP would hit a hidden, submerged rock along the shore, it was a quick and exciting way to go from standing to swimming. If I were to put myself in danger by straying too far from the shoreline, nearer to the large fishing boats, it would feel like David against Goliath. However, a shining path—the glimmering, road-like refection that the waning full moon created on the water guided me—each and every time.

I can remember where I was when I first heard someone use the poetic words, "the shining path." It was Perú in the mid-eighties where I was traveling, but they weren't describing moonbeam on the ocean; they were referring to a Maoist-inspired communist guerrilla group fighting the government forces, named Sendero Luminoso—the Shining Path.

Peru's first communist party leader, Jose Carlos Mariátegui, philosophized that "Marxism-Leninism will open the Shining Path to revolution."

But instead, the Shining Path opened a twenty-year civil war. That, along with the government's counter-insurgency left as many as 60,000 people dead. The violence and terrorism included attacks on common people, as well as government officials, with weekly bombs exploding in front of police stations, on highways, and in towns.

While traveling there, I encountered the military checkpoints in the countryside of Perú. The soldiers with large guns in hand couldn't figure me out. I was young—nineteen years old—and traveling alone. I would show up in the back of a truck with campesinos and goats in a sparsely populated war zone, carrying nothing but books in Spanish about Krishna Consciousness, and Octavio Paz poetry, with one Churchill body surfing fin. Today, I can understand their fear and confusion. They were terrorized by the bombs, as everybody was.

Once, I was detained at a checkpoint high in the mountains for six hours. One soldier, certain I was somehow helping Sendero Luminoso, peppered me with questions, while the other guy just laughed maniacally, drunk on Pisco Sour and Coca leaves. From my bag, they pulled out the bodysurfing fin. Confused, they became ludicrously convinced I was using it to somehow booby-trap the river bridges with explosives.

I had a surprisingly challenging time explaining the obvious. That something as innocuous as a surf-fin, used to swim and play in the ocean, was not a subversive device aiding in a violent rebel uprising.

I bought the bodysurfing fin from a kid in Miraflores along the coast so I could be in the ocean and bodysurf if I came across some waves.

In spite of the world around me, I felt safe, cloaked by an unseen, benevolent force field. I had my books and my one surf-fin—my safety blankets. I was on a spiritual quest. I convinced the soldiers that I was harmless, and ultimately, they released me.

Reminiscing about my 1985 Peruvian travels provided some diversion as I paddled on the Sea of Cortez, helping me pass the time in my mind instead of focusing my attention on the aches and pains in my body.

In Perú, I was on what Joseph Campbell would call a *hero's journey*. In his book, *The Power of Myth*, Joseph Campbell talked about how, "We're so engaged in doing things to achieve purposes of outer value, that we forget the inner-value, the rapture, that is associated with being alive."

I was still on the same path, now paddling to Cabo Pulmo—a path to know myself, to be myself. A path to go from the known world to the unknown world. To seek rapture. To seek all the world beneath my feet, my board, my paddle, has to offer.

Like the first white snow flowers of spring, the planets Venus and Jupiter were now visible in the southeastern sky. Slowly, they began to rise, the first indications that the sun is forthcoming.

With the good news of the approaching sunrise also came the bad news that my left thumb was now cramping, which made holding on to the paddle on my left side more difficult. Instead of wrapping my thumb around the paddle, I laid it on the outside of the paddle grip, which unfortunately provided less-efficient strokes, but more importantly, was less painful.

With the sky starting to lighten, I could now see the silhouette of my despair. The boats I've been seeing all night are indeed shrimp trawlers. A new day dawns with a purple, indigo blue, and now red sky, but the same old thieves pillage the sea.

Years ago, the shrimp trawlers plundered the northern Sea of Cortez waters until the fishery there collapsed, and now they're here doing the same thing—same old story, but different time and place.

Bottom trawling, as it's called, uses heavily weighted nets that drag across the ocean floor, from shallow coastal waters to the extreme depth of 6,000 feet. Shrimp trawling is one of the most indiscriminate forms of fishing, shredding whatever stands in its way, tearing into her... and tearing into us. For every pound of wild shrimp caught, trawlers kill as much as 40 pounds of by-catch.

The boats' weighted nets drag along her floor to capture the shrimp, but they also scoop up everything else in their path, including coral reefs or rocks where fish hide from predators, sea grasses, fish, starfish, turtles, seabirds and even sharks and marine mammals are all captured and discarded by bottom trawling. Shrimp trawling is comparable to bulldozing an entire section of rainforest to catch a single species of bird.

Back and forth I watched the boats go.

I paddled out, away from the raw shoreline I'd been clinging to during the night, veering my path to intersect with the stern of the industrial shrimp trawler for a closer view.

The crew of three men looked like the product of a week-long alcoholic bender—scruffy, threadbare clothes, unshaven, red eyes, and cagey looks. They clutched a part of her—the ocean trapped in the trawl net on the starboard side of the boat. They looked as bulldozed as their "catch." I was beat—from paddling, from watching the ocean get ransacked by fishermen, from the mindless consumption of a sleepwalking society eating shrimp kabobs off the barbeque.

Overwhelming majorities of the people in our Baja community feel like I do, that the shrimp trawlers are like pirates pillaging our ocean. Yet the vast majority of the community continues to support the abhorrent destruction

– by buying and eating the shrimp. It is our consumption that drives all forms of legal and illegal fishing. The question I often ask myself is, how do we wake up people who are, as Desmond Tutu says, *"Only pretending to be asleep"*?

These old, tired ways of the world have a bad ending. Boris Worm, a marine ecologist and an associate professor of marine conservation biology at Dalhousie University in Halifax, Canada, says that if humans keep fishing at the current pace, there will be no more fish left in the oceans by 2048.

The levels of violence and destruction are stunning. We kill literally billions of sea animals yearly, mostly by suffocation—but sometimes by bodily decompression, or simply being crushed to death under the weight of other dying fish.

An alarming example of how bottom trawling and gillnet fishing is pushing species to the brink of extinction is the plight of the Vaquita porpoise in the northern Sea of Cortez. The Vaquita is the most endangered cetacean in the world. With an estimate released in March 2019, only 22 individuals remain in existence. In a desperate attempt to save the few remaining vaquitas, Sea Shepherd Conservation Society is working in alliance with the Mexican navy to remove the illegal gillnets as soon as they are seen, on a daily basis. Absent these efforts to address the root of the problem, our consumption is what drives this form of destruction.

I turned the corner of the easternmost point of the Baja peninsula, Punta Arena—Lighthouse Point. I turned away from the shrimp trawlers, away from the destruction.

White egrets crisscrossed the curving shoreline. The North wind breathed ever so slightly, forcing me to paddle exclusively on the right side to keep the bow of my board tracking correctly along the coast.

I was drained physically from the long journey, and mentally from thinking about the violence. I lowered myself to my knees on my SUP board, head down and overwhelmed. I am just one person I thought to myself, what could I possibly do?

A fragrant breeze burst from onshore, invoking the sound of a tambourine. The warming sun, an offshore wind. With it brought the aroma of a mango tree and mesquite smoke with the omnipresent smell of corn tortillas on the stove. In México, *Sin maíz, no hay país. Without corn, there is no country.* The smell of corn tortillas smelled like home.

Unfortunately, traveling with a mini-stove burner on my SUP, hand-patting tortillas clearly isn't realistic. But the far-fetched idea amused me and lightened my overly serious mood. So, I sat and refueled with a sensible peanut butter-cacao-banana sandwich, daydreaming about warm tortillas with mango juice.

I thought, of course, of Carol.

In all likelihood, she was watching the same sunrise from our warm home, seeing those same colors in the sky. No matter where we are—even when we're seemingly worlds apart—we sit by the same sea, the same waves, the same heart.

I looked down the coast to the boundary of Cabo Pulmo to her protected waters and my ultimate destination. The food, the sight of Cabo Pulmo, and my thoughts of home all soothed any lingering despair. My paddle entered the water with more purpose with each stroke.

Outrigger paddle technique I learned as a kid in Hawai'i informs my present-day technique and focus. In plain language, the less splashing sounds from my paddle in the water, the more efficient my strokes can be. I reached forward and pulled myself to the paddle, repeating it over and over again: left side, right side ...

With my focus on the bow of my board and the surrounding ocean, the passing of my hands and paddle in front of me pacified my forward vision, as if it were some form of undiscovered treatment for Post-Traumatic Stress Disorder.

Turkey vultures and frigates found a column of rising mid-morning air above Las Lagunas as the Mobula rays leapt out of the water around me. I arrived in Las Barracas, the boundary of Cabo Pulmo, with a new blister on my right index finger, and my left foot was going numb.

Pleasure and suffering motivated behavior for all of us, from soaring birds and breaching rays, to surfers like myself.

I rested intermittently, sitting on my board to get feeling back in my feet, forcing myself to enjoy the ebb and flow reverie of endurance paddling on the Sea of Cortez. In pleasure or in pain, I try to give neither free rein.

Turning my attention to the ocean again, I envisioned the sentient life below my board. A nesting Puffer fish building a mandala designed home in the sand—a yellow reef fish taking shelter in a familiar sea anemone. Other fish, like the purple Anthias watching for predators with the ability to see a broader color range than we can ever see. Mexican Groupers that use body shimmies and head gestures to invite Moray Eels to cooperate on a hunt together.

Many fish court prior to mating, getting in the mood with playful passes against each other's bodies. Dorados show the ultimate commitment of companionship by mating for life. Individual recognition is common among all species of marine animals, recognizing each other by facial patterns whether camouflaged or not.

The consciousness of her watery depths living and breathing below me was undeniable, yet some people only want to see the vacant stare of glassy-eyed, soulless fish at the end of their fishing line, or pressed against the seascape in their nets, or on their plates dressed in a decorative garnish.

The ocean has always been a part of me. I am her passionate and awestruck devotee. I contain the memory of her in my cells, encoded into my surfer DNA. She is a part of me.

I recognize my true self when I hear her waves, or when I see the sparkle of moonbeam on her watery surface. She is a part of every living thing. Her life force affects every aspect of life on Earth: influencing the weather, regulating the atmosphere and the temperature, shaping culture, shaping us by the vastness of her heart.

Every major event I have had is shared with the ocean. When a child is born in our family, I celebrate by going surfing. When a friend gets married, I surf after the ceremony. When a loved one dies, I go to her to find solace. There are too many days in my life to count that I've sat next to my younger brother Jim while surfing in her waters. In big waves, small waves, for a celebration and during grief, we surf together.

Following our father's death in San Diego, in our twenties, we found ourselves in the ocean surfing the Cardiff Reef after his memorial service. We couldn't think of a better place to connect with Dad, to connect with ourselves, than in her waves.

We let her tender embrace do its job. We discovered that we weren't heavy stones that would sink to the bottom when tossed into her watery depths. We floated.

In her waters, we found equilibrium. The waves made sense when the world didn't—a haven where we were okay—a refuge where we were able to smile again. The tender wounds of our sadness reshaped into a workable self to navigate on land again.

She was our shining path.

I paddled toward Punta Pulmo with a sudden burst of emotion, a moment of bliss, the joy of unity. Maybe it's a paddler's high from paddling twelve hours straight, or simply the feeling of gratitude for family and friends.

The lows can be low, but the highs can be even higher with endurance paddling. The endorphins generated can arrive from out of the blue and shoot through the stratosphere.

I was buzzing. I had an overwhelming feeling of connectedness with all things, a sensation of deep belonging—to the ocean and to the land that shapes her.

A shining path of moonbeam led me to this moment. I felt the sun above me, and I saw the ripples of water around my board as extensions of myself. I could sense the strength of the calcium carbonate in sand dollars and in coral, and I felt the weightlessness of the clouds in the sky. I was, at once, everything and nothing.

But in an instant, the mystical moment was gone, I lost grip of my paddle and, inexplicably, my wristwatch popped off my wrist into the waters below. Ker plunk. Gone to the depths. I watched it tumble in curious disbelief. Like a fighter plane shot from the sky, my watch spiraled down into the deep blue water. Ninety-five feet of water swallowed time. I laughed out loud at the strange symbolism and at the bad luck I have with watches.

In grade school, at eight years old, I had a strange attraction to watches, specifically other kids' watches. It culminated one day when I stole a watch from a kid named Dave. I never got caught, and I never gave the watch back. Don't ask me how I stole the watch, I don't remember. Neither do I know why I stole the watch, other than it was shiny, it made a ticking sound, and it was in Dave's possession, not mine. Ever since then, the karmic imprint has followed me.

This watch that just fell off my wrist is at least the third watch I'd donated to the Sea of Cortez. Not to mention the other watches I've either lost or ruined by dropping into paint buckets, or any variety of other means and ways to lose or destroy a watch. I've done it all. They're not expensive watches, but neither are they cheap. They're your average surf-dive watches. These damn watches get ripped off my wrist while kite-surfing, or simply fall off my wrist as this one did, without any impact at all. I attribute all of my bad luck with watches to my eight-year-old self who stole little Davie Henderson's watch.

Neither am I too pleased that my watch, now settled in the depths, was yet another piece of trash that could possibly cause harm to her vibrant life she nurtures so sweetly. I never want to do damage to the one I hold so dearly.

You might be wondering, as Carol had, why do I need a watch while surfing and paddling on the ocean? Well, I wanted to know how long I'd been surfing, or what time to come in for dinner, or simply how long it takes to paddle forty miles to Cabo Pulmo! The irony that I am still a captive of time in the timelessness of the ocean does not escape me.

As I paddled the last two miles, past the far outer reef onto the second reef closer to shore, I had officially arrived—and without my watch, I had no idea how long it took for me to get here.

I slipped into the sublime waters. In the buoyancy, she released me. My arms and legs were spread like a starfish. I felt hope. *El que busca encuentra – One finds what one looks for.* Here, the ocean was protected from fishing, safe from harm. We rested in each other.

When I can see a vision actualized, I can picture the possibilities. In this case, the marine sanctuary of Cabo

Pulmo turned things around. They stopped the insanity of overfishing on their part of the coast. And where there is possibility, there is hope. Perhaps one day, more of the lifeblood of this planet will be protected.

Floating on my back I could hear the crackling flora and fauna of the reef below me. The sound of the reef is the lyrical language of the ancient One. Underwater, the reef sounded like small pebbles being poured into sand—a constant crackling.

A picture can tell a story of a thousand words, but the sounds I was hearing could tell a story of a thousand pictures. The story is about thousands of fish living on a healthy coral reef. I gravitated to its poetry and rolled over face down, opening myself to the mysteries she was willing to share … and I dove twelve feet down to the reef below. Without goggles, my vision was blurred by saline, but life was all around me. I could hear it. I could feel it. She surrounded me.

A multitude of snapping shrimp; the frothing, mating chorus of fish; the bubbling sounds from small crustaceans; even the moaning song of distant humpback whales could be heard as it echoed across the reef.

Many of these fish use this cacophonic chorus of the reef to find their way back home.

Returning to the surface, absorbed in the vastness of her presence, I indulged myself in a familiar daydream. We finally put violence against one another and against the Earth aside. And instead of killing the ocean, by taking, and taking, and taking, we instead choose to receive two of her most essential and unexpected gifts—hope and inspiration.

The day before Dr. Martin Luther King was assassinated, in his compelling "I've been to the Mountaintop" speech, he declared, "The choice before us is no longer violence or nonviolence; it's nonviolence or nonexistence. That is where we're at today."

Hopelessly an optimist, I chose the path with the glimmering, road-like refection the waning full moon created on her silky surface—the Shining Path.

I closed my eyes and uttered one of the simplest prayers I knew: *Help.*

Chapter 4

THE WAY OF WATER

I was landlocked—at a blinking red traffic light on the
lonesome side San Quintín, México. No books, no compass,
only the bells of passing goats. I sipped my early morning
tea in a to-go mug. It was still dark. I rubbed the sleep out
of eyes. On the radio, an old Woody Guthrie song played. I
was feeling the pang of solitude from yesterday's solo surf
trip to Salsipuedes, a legendary surf spot north of
Ensenada.

I was driven out of the precious waters by the rank,
contaminating smells from the nearby floating fish farms.
These farms are the fishing industry's ocean version of land-
based factory farming—confinement, overcrowding, waste
run-off, and pollution.

The smells of pollution at Salsipuedes, in our ocean—the

lifeblood of our planet—set a melancholy tone from yesterday. I heard three deep gongs from the church bells in the center of town. I was feeling a little *bound to lose, no good to nobody, and no good for nothing.* And yet, I was in no particular hurry. There was only one way for me to get to the other side of melancholy. As Robert Frost said, "The best way out is always through."

It's easy to be happy when her waters are clean and pristine; there are good waves to surf, an abundance of ocean life under my surfboard to connect with, and Carol is with me. The other day I opened my notebook to see the words I had written—*Note to self: write more haiku while in the hammock.*

What words flow through me into my notebook when her waters are polluted, or if there are no waves to surf? Or when I have a flat tire on the highway, or if a local Mexican cop shakes me down, or when I'm not with Carol and my heart feels like a pair of tumbling shoes in the Laundromat dryer? How do I respond when I feel the pangs of loneliness, doubt, or despair?

Happiness is not a destination. It's a journey.

As I pasted through San Quintín, I planned on stopping when the sun comes up at an uninhabited beach break called Socorro for ocean time—time in her waters—a quick surf, or simply time to spend sitting on the shore, a moment of restoration before heading further south for more surf. To touch water. To connect.

Water adapts to make anyplace perfect for itself, settling at the low spots, or eddying swiftly around high spots, always with natural timing to move. I learn something new from water every time I'm near, or in water.

The streets of San Quintín were bustling. No longer were there herds of goats wearing bells around their necks strolling the countryside. A surprising number of cars are already out on the road in the pre-dawn gloom of the city.

There was a forlorn side street billboard advertising a hamburger while objectifying women and promoting messy eating all at once. I'm not sure if that's supposed to be blood or ketchup dripping down the side of her mouth. The sport of trivializing a women's worth is outdone only by our blood thirst for killing and eating animals.

It's like Bizarro World. Life in the middle of San Quintín is on the opposite schedule of the rest of the world. The busyness is too much for my sleepy mind.

At the tope—a Mexican speed bump, a friendly, well-dressed red-cross worker thanked me for my 20 Peso donation. *"Buenos Días...gracias...que vaya bien!"* The red-cross workers cheerful words tumbled into the car window, startling me out of my morning stupor.

Then, out of the corner of my eye, I saw him. A filthy, dirty street dog, as he nonchalantly hopped off the curb. He was the kind of dog you would see snuggled and held under someone's arm in the United States, and many other parts of the world. It's a tough life to be born a street-dog in México.

He could have been a Shih Tzu mix. I've always had trouble saying the word, Shih Tzu, without waiting for someone to say Gesundheit after.

Nevertheless, this little fella was about one-foot tall and probably weighed no more than five pounds. He was wearing the hardships of life in his tangled, dirty hair. He personified the look of how I felt, *bound to lose, no good to nobody, and no good for nothing.*

And suddenly, without a second thought, he veered from the curbside and turned into the road and toward what I am certain would be his imminent death. But his head was raised upward and he had a cavalier swagger to his step. It's not the look of the downtrodden. No glance to the left. No glance to the right. His certainty of safety was larger than his stature.

Believe it or not, many Mexican dogs seem to have learned to look both ways before crossing the street. They seem to understand cars and recognize danger. But I sense a bad outcome here. This little guy was too small to be seen. He was about to become a Mexican speed bump.

I had seen other dogs hit and killed by cars—a dog hit by a taxi ahead of us on the road in southern Baja; another one on a rainy, dark highway in Northern California. But none more traumatic than to witness my dog Shadow being killed ahead of me when I was a kid skateboarding down our street in Southern California when I was a kid.

In fact, I was lucky to come out unscathed on that one. At the last second, I swerved to the left and missed the front fender of the car by inches. But I didn't feel fortunate because at that very same moment, I witnessed my little buddy Shadow run directly under the front wheel of the car.

The fragility of life accepts boundless heartbreak.

Loud buses were kicking dust into the Mexican morning air. Broken mufflers on nearby cars were drowning out my car horn. I was now laying on the horn with my two hands, elbows raised, lifting myself out of my seat from the effort. "Look out!" I yelled instinctively, realizing I had better yell out in Spanish, "Aguas, aguas!" But my windows were rolled up. Neither the drivers of the cars nor the little dog could hear my desperation. The curly-haired dog looked cherubic as he cooly, casually strolled into traffic, blissfully unaware of the apocalypse around him. He hadn't a care in the world.

Then I saw it. He was carrying a small stuffed animal in his mouth. At least I thought it was a stuffed animal. The toy was dangling a bit out the sides of his mouth, but firmly in his grasp. I could see it more clearly now. Yes, it was a small teddy bear.

This little guy carrying a teddy bear with him into the busy Mexican street was the epitome of the expression, *Querer es poder. Where there's a will, there's a way.*

To my astonishment, by sheer luck of timing, or the unseen mysterious ways of the universe, a path cleared in the traffic for the dog to cross the street.

One car went ahead of the dog, another car turned off the road at just the right time, and the rest of traffic moved as if divinely orchestrated around the dog. It was the equivalent of paddling across the inside section of the big-wave spot, Las Islas de Todos Santos, without even getting wet. The crashing waves in the form of cement trucks, motorbikes, old buses, and cars were all around, but onward the little dog calmly trotted.

I appeared to be the only person to have even noticed or reacted to the miracle dog crossing the darkened street. But there it was, a path through the waves.

Did the dog hear the distant church bells informing him that it was safe to cross the street? Perhaps it was the invisible force field of a teddy bear in his mouth. It was nothing short of a miracle. I wanted to follow the little guy after he made it safely across the street and into the neighborhood. I wanted to congratulate him, to care for him, to know him.

I felt like I had witnessed something extraordinary. I wanted to give him some food and clean him up. I wanted to tell him about the Woody Guthrie song I was listening to. I wanted to learn the secret of life from him. How did he do that? Casually and confidently cross a busy road with the expectation that, contrary to all visible evidence, it was indeed a friendly universe?

Just as I turned the corner to follow him, he slipped under a metal fence, like water down a hill. He scuttled past a mechanic's shop that looked more like a junk yard, and then around the corner of a grey cement block home with rebar sticking up out of the roof. Gone. He was out of sight. Staying low and opportunistic, like the vital quality of water. Finding the slightest opening to pass through while the opening is present, this little Zen-dog has a well-worn path across the streets and through the neighborhood.

Nothing in this world is softer or weaker than water. It is humble, never drawing attention to itself, never asking for acknowledgment.

And there is nothing stronger and more determined than water. In spite of any obstacle along its path, its arrival to its destination always seems effortless.

We should all move through this world with as much ease and grace as water, and as this little dog.

As I drove away from San Quintín, I passed a tomato processing-plant, and several yards of scrapheap. A burn-pile smoldered. The smell of burning cardboard and eucalyptus drifted through my car window. The road began to narrow toward the coastline, pointing me in a crooked line.

It's like that—a circuitous journey into grace—curves and dips in the road. Earlier this morning, I was only focused on the desolateness of this world. I was missing the little miracles of life within the bleakness. I was overlooking the unexpected life around me.

A little dog lifted my vision. I'm not *bound to lose, no good to nobody, and no good for nothing.*

My companion was the 6'4" *fish* surfboard strapped on top of the car. Our ocean was in view and sparkled on the right side of the highway. We were heading south. I looked forward to feeling the waves, her healing waters at Socorro later this morning.

The Tao Te Ching, an ancient poem from Chinese philosopher Lao Tzu describes how water is the way of life. "The highest good is like water, which nourishes all things without trying to. It is content with the low places that people disdain."

The simple element of water allows my spirit to thrive in the ocean. It often takes me on odd paths, circuitous ones—with occasional lonesome surf excursions.

I don't have all of the answers in life. I never will. And I'm overly prone to despair. I know that about myself. I've learned this lesson before. To adapt to the declivities—the ups and downs of life. To move, like water with ease around obstacles. Water doesn't complain about the path it follows; it simply follows the path and moves when it needs to.

I don't need large, cataclysmic shifts. There's no need for a Moses-sized revelation by seeing God in a burning bush. Water goes unnoticed, but it's relentless. It remains still, or it never stops. Its force is a manifestation of its nature. It never tries to be something it is not.

I had been given a teaching this morning. A little, dusty, curly-haired Shih Tzu-street-dog, holding a teddy bear in his mouth, living in the rough part of San Quintín, México was my teacher.

Surfing, in its purist form, is an effort to mimic water, to be like a wave. This Mexican street dog who lives amongst the dangers of our harsh world knows the way of water.

1. *Be proud and go with ease and determination.*
2. *Stay low and humble.*
3. *Flow, and enjoy the ride.*

Chapter 5

THE NET

The moment after I frantically ripped open the heavy, black industrial fishing net to free the beautiful blue Jackfish, I regretted it. My remorse surprised me. How could helping liberate fish about to die from this buoyed net be wrong?

In a passionate, impulsive flash, I launched myself into an existential juggernaut about the morality of monkey wrenching for the greater good.

Early in the clean washed shine of a songbird morning, I grabbed my stand-up paddleboard. Birds chattered in the guava tree behind our house. The scent of guava was thick in the air. A Gila woodpecker was drilling holes into a coconut palm. It's humid in Baja for November. Remnant clouds from a tropical storm lingered in the mountains. Three large raindrops fall. Seconds later, sunshine. This continues: three drops of rain, then nothing. It was just enough to make me look up with expectation of heavier rain to come.

Lattice sunlight seeped through clouds as I stepped onto my SUP in the Sea of Cortez. As I started paddling north, I connected with the original life force of Planet Earth: water. I rode the ocean's conveyer belt as Stevie Wonder's song, "Living for The City," blasted through my earphones. The crank and rhythm of efficient paddle strokes on my SUP intent on going for distance. The song lyrics were juxtaposed to the calming ocean around me.

Surrounded by four walls that ain't so pretty...
Living just enough, just enough for the city...

The ocean felt like freedom. No walls.

I paddled past a green turtle with old man facial features, and Mexican manta rays, with fancy white polka dots on their wings. Both species flew underwater away from the shadow my board projected on the ocean floor, forty feet below.

Fleeing, their movements looked like leaves in the wind. All the images shape-shifted on the textured surface of the ocean. Her beauty was below me. Her beauty was above me. And her beauty was all around me.

I was a part of that beauty and that beauty was a part of me. It calmed my breathing and slowed my heart rate. The freedom I felt from that beauty was like something that needed to be given back, a gift exchange. Not just to take in. Not just to look upon.

There it was, like a flashing red light announcing danger, a red buoy a quarter-mile off shore, with a spherical commercial fishing net draped below. I stumbled upon a sinkhole in the boundless beauty of the ocean. In the net, there are hundreds of blue Jackfish swimming in endless, torturous circles, looking for a way out. The weak ones are gasping at the surface—on their sides—dying of confusion and fatigue.

I couldn't un-see what was in front of me. I couldn't simply paddle away.

Their eyes in the net seem fixed on me, their mouths opening and closing, as if gasping for freedom. How could I not do something? How could I not respond to these beautiful creatures—my friends, my tribe, my heart?

I thought back to that cove in Hawai'i where I was spearfishing when I was thirteen years old—that magnificent Triggerfish who swam over to me. I discovered my real self when seeing her. By not taking her life that day, she ended up giving me mine. The life I know. The kindness of that moment with her unfolded the path of my life—the path of kindness. I've carried that moment with me ever since.

I had my board, my paddle, and my oceanic heart. The path of kindness led me here. How could I not respond to the fish's certain death in this commercial fishing net?

It would be only a matter of time for them, swimming in panicked loops below to start dying as the one's above are. I feel their distress. So much life tangled up in the sea. Their suffering becomes our suffering.

I had seen these nets before in other locations, but never with so many animals trapped, nightmarishly confined, and never without fishermen in sight.

Looking at the red, spherical commercial fishing net in front of me, my heart was sick from sadness and anger. Sadness and anger together is a strong mix, a strong cocktail. The sadness came from seeing the suffering of the fish—the confusion—the dying. The anger comes from seeing the destruction, our blindness, and our delusion of separateness that creates these commercial fishing nets in the first place.

My hand reached into the net and found a seam to tear open before my mind had an opportunity to consider the situation. There is a Mexican proverb: *Haz el bien y no veas a quien – Do good and don't worry to whom.*

The fulfillment of seeing their escape to freedom was satisfying beyond words. I could feel their relief as they escaped.

Some fish leapt toward the opening with an opportunistic burst of energy. Other fish, drowning on their sides, sick and dying from confusion from what is known as Cryptic Stress Response, the fishes' biochemical overload from high levels of stress from capture. The fish could barely move toward the hole in the net I madly tore open. For those precious fish, I helped by hand placing them out of the net and into freedom—as many of them as I could. I ripped the net some more. Laboriously capturing the sick ones. Gently delivering them back to life—the open ocean.

Hundreds of the other fish still trapped and unaware of the newly created exit hole swam deeper into the grasp of the net. Those fish were also trying to escape, but were confused by my presence hovering above them, hovering above the net.

The deepening Baja sky releasing droplets of water rippling the surface of the sea.

Here is where I arrived at the crux of the dilemma. The commercial fishing net is wrong, but what I'm doing isn't right.

Thich Nhat Hanh has fourteen Buddhist precepts for engaged Buddhism. He articulated what I already knew. Several of them are:

1. Do not kill. Do not let others kill. Find whatever means possible to protect life and prevent war.

2. Possess nothing that should belong to others. Respect the property of others, but prevent others from profiting from human suffering or the suffering of other species on Earth.

Daniel Pauly, a marine biologist well known for work in studying human impact on global fisheries—including here in the Sea of Cortez—describes the world's governments as having a "fishing-industrial complex," a Ponzi scheme that will leave the future generations with a fishless ocean. Some 394,819 fish were killed globally in the ten seconds it took for you to read this sentence.

Scientists are our modern-day wisdom-keepers like the Nez Perce Indian wisdom keepers warning their people of the white man coming with guns and disease. These scientists are painting a grim picture of our future, but we're too distracted by Trump's tweets, the new iPhone, Kim Kardashian's new outfit, or conspiracy theories.

We are literally eating ourselves out of house and home. The ocean is being emptied like a sugary pixie stick into the mouth of a child.

However, ripping holes in all the fishing nets is not the solution. It does nothing about the demand side of the equation. Fishermen pull fish from their home on a daily basis to supply the public's demand to consume. It's the public's appetite, not the fishermen, that are to blame for the existence of these nets.

Not to mention the fact that my ripping holes in fishing nets would also make for some very pissed off fishermen. And after ripping a hole in this net, and watching many of the fish escape, the angry fishermen scenario is what worried me the most.

I live down the beach from this location. I know many of the fishermen that live here, and they know me. Some of them are my neighbors. We see each other in the neighborhood, or miles off-shore—them fishing, me paddling.

To them, I'm the gringo surfer.

We are friends. If they discovered I was the person who damaged their equipment and released their catch they would no longer be friendly to me. They would be angry with me, and from their perspective, justifiably so.

After all, I am breaking the law. And I suppose some of
them might even want to hurt me. In that situation, the
best-case scenario for me would be to be in jail, where I
would be safer. And in a jail in México I would be
Surrounded by four walls that ain't so pretty.

With these thoughts swirling around my head, I stopped
trying to open the net. I knew it isn't right. My grief for the
dear, helpless fish remaining in the net seems endless. The
thought of leaving all those souls is excruciating and felt
wrong. But I had to. They were trapped and would die, as
are literally millions of other fish every day.

Before paddling back home I need to consider my path.

It is a new path. No longer was I alone buoyed upon my
own wobbly surfboard to carry me. The numbers—the
vastness of life—held me afloat.

I feel as awakened as if my hair were on fire. I need to do
something, anything, to rouse our sleepwalking society; to
conserve our ocean; to protect her as if our whole existence
depends upon it.

We are part of a larger picture, no better than, no worse than others. Albert Einstein said it beautifully:

"A human being is part of a whole, called by us the "Universe," a part limited in time and space. He experiences himself, his thoughts and feelings, as something separated from the rest — a kind of optical delusion of his consciousness.... Our task must be to free ourselves from this prison by widening our circles of compassion to embrace all living creatures and the whole of nature in its beauty."

I took a moment of silence to sit on my board with my eyes closed. But what is silence? Her waters toggle my board, the seagulls cawing, an osprey whistles. Bird sounds chronicle their presence. They exist. They are real. They matter. Their happiness is our happiness. How could it not be?

Some voices we recognize. The sound of our own name. The bird's daily, daring declaration breaks the night's darkness to announce, I am here. Do you hear me? I am here. My name is the sound of me. Every moment of silence is the spaciousness of our names returning to us. An echo.

THE NET

Who would we be in a world without birds? Who would we be with an ocean without fish?

I slipped off my board into the ocean and propelled myself just below the surface to listen to the silence. Yet, it too is full of sound—the sounds of life—the richness of bubbles, and the sounds of the crackling, living coral reef. The beating of my heart is like the fish announcing their names. I am here and you are here. We are here.

For each and every fish trapped in the net, I counted the heartbeats of my anguishing heart. One, two, three, four, five, six, seven… counting until my breath is spent from sorrow.

There are too many souls trapped in the net for me to count. And not enough human hearts in the world that beat for the ones trapped in nets. Most of us humans are trapped in their own nets, unable to see what we do to the world around us. And unable to see what we do to the world within us.

I am daunted by the enormity of this world's self-inflicted grief.

I dive down past where I ripped a hole in the fishing net, upside down to our world of incarcerations—upside down to our world of captivities.

The precious fish swam faster circles in the net the deeper I went, moving away from me, trying to escape their entrapment. Thirty-five feet deep, their eyes searched me for my humanity.

Freedom for ourselves can only be true if we value freedom for others as well. What kind of freedom is it if it doesn't include freedom for those who don't look like us?

My soul drowned momentarily in the net with the fish. My intense sadness pulled me back to the surface. I surfed and paddled my way back home—away from here, or back to here. It's all in the same direction. The healing ocean sounds splashing off my SUP paddle cannot change this moment into something else, into something other than what it is.

There are too many vulnerable worlds that are infringed upon. Too many voices unheard. Too many of us are drowning in the nets we've cast.

Every day, we make delicate decisions of right and wrong.

THE NET

My decision to leave that net, abandoning those remaining precious individuals, seared a permanent, salty imprint on my grieving heart.

Chapter 6

A RED BANDANA

Some people have the impression that I am a laid-back person, but those people have not looked closely enough at my eyes. My eyes are not the timeless, dreamy eyes of an enlightened Samadhi. Nope. Mine can project some pretty serious stink-eye, which is of course, the opposite of laid-back. *Stinkeye - Echar mal de ojo*! I can throw a stink-eye as far as a quarter of a mile down the beach when necessary.

Even a 92-year-old man named Stan—a twenty-year neighbor of mine who can barely walk—is a member in my stink-eye club.

Stan greets me in the mornings with, "Hello sir." He personifies some sort of bold, lone-wolf stoicism and the megalomania of Captain Ahab from Herman Melville's Moby Dick.

On this hot June day, Stan pulled off his red bandana from around his neck and soaked it in ice water to stay cool in the stifling Baja sun.

As he rubbed his white whiskers, he asked me, "You going surfing today?"

I smiled. I'd been surfing now for over 40 years and I'm still excited about the thought of it. I started to answer Stan's question, but he didn't have his hearing aids in and he didn't wait long enough for me to respond.

"Well, I'm gonna see if the fish are biting today," he said.

He's holding his fishing pole, which for the moment is doubling as a walking stick keeping him upright. My morning tea was getting cold, so I told him that I'll be nearby if he needs any help walking.

I was glad to slip away from a conversation with Stan. Stan will hunt, fish, and kill anything that moves. Yesterday, he wore me out in conversation about his account of dove shooting in the mountains. Dove shooting. This evidently is something people do for fun. Yes, the same lovely doves, whose cooing voices and songs visit me in my garden as they cautiously bathe in the birdbath, bringing with them serenity and life, Stan kills for the fun of it. He says, "I don't even get out of the truck. I just shoot 'em from the passenger's seat."

The high, thin clouds in the melancholy sky turned pink and purple from the rising sun. I was glad I brought my notepad with me to watch the otherworldly sunrise. Thinking of the-Stans-of-this-world, I could feel some angst-filled scribbling coming on. I plopped myself down on the granite rock seawall along the beach, the place of my exile. Tiny black ants marched in line along the granite seawall to points unknown from points unknown. A few occasionally detour off path to explore my leg, so I gently offered the back of my hand and a whoosh of my breath to relocate them again. The ant relocation project happens seldom enough, not requiring me to relocate myself yet.

As I watched Stan shuffle his way to the shoreline with the red bandana around his neck, I couldn't help but think of Clavel.

Clavel was a deer my parents rescued from Esqueda, México. Clavel also wore a red bandana. We figured if he escaped from our yard, he needed something to identify himself so people would know that he was not a wild deer, he was with us. A red-bandana-wearing homeboy from a poor Mexican border-town was now living the good life in our backyard in Southern California.

People would walk by our house with surprise seeing a deer in our backyard and would shout to us, "Quick, kids! Get your parents! There's a deer trapped in your backyard!" We would tell them not to worry; he lives with us. "See the red bandana?"

Recently, I asked my mother for her recollections of Clavel's life, and I found her account of events far less interesting than my own. Proving that truth usually lies somewhere between our inherently skewed memory of it, and reality. Sure, we had some overlapping remembrances, but as it turns out, my mind seems to be a tad more susceptible to hyperbole.

Our memories fool us. Neuroscience suggests that the more we remember an event, the more we change that event in our minds. So, evidently I am a hopeless fabulist.

Once, at a gathering as a child, I heard my father introduce himself as an Irishmen, born in Tijuana. Neither the ethnicity nor the location was true, so I suppose my sense of realism doesn't fall too far from the Tijuana mango tree.

My father was an adventurous, free-spirited businessman with a humanitarian streak. He owned a small four-seater airplane and would, on occasion, fly doctors and dentists into rural parts of México to help people with health issues and dental work. One of the locations we visited more than once was Esqueda, Lupita's hometown. Lupita was a babysitter for my sister, my brother, and me in California. She was wonderful.

As a kid in Los Angeles, I remember seeing a hailstorm outside for the first time, which is a rare event in Los Angeles. At the time, I didn't even know the word for hail in English, no less Spanish. It was magical to hear Lupita refer to the hail as *"Granizo, que milagro, granizo!"* *Hail, what a miracle, hail!* The white pellets of the hailstorm bounced off the green lawn like a trampoline. It was a *milagro* of nature, language, and love at the front door holding Lupita's hand.

I can also remember my disbelief at hearing the hardships of Lupita's life, including how one of her adult sons drowned in a river he was crossing. He didn't know how to swim, which in itself was inconceivable to me.

On this particular trip to Esqueda, the dentist treated a man with only a hodge-podge assortment of teeth in his mouth. After fixing his tooth, or pulling his tooth—whichever—the man explained to my father that he was caring for a young, rescued deer. A deer orphaned by hunters. He asked my father for help.

I've lived in México off and on for much of my life. Rural México, back in the 70s, was very rustic—meaning little electricity, few indoor bathrooms, and little economic opportunity.

This man in the rural town of Esqueda, México who rescued this deer has always been an extraordinary person for me to reflect upon. At his job, he earned four dollars a day and was not able to afford dental work, yet he took in and cared for another mouth to feed—a wild baby deer.

Jack Kerouac wrote, "One man practicing kindness in the wilderness is worth all the temples this world pulls."

Compassion moves us in unexplainable ways. It can be paradoxical and illogical. It very well might be the height of spiritual expression. This man was struggling to survive, so reaching out to us Gringos for help made perfect sense.

I glanced up from my notepad to see Stan. He was the antithesis of the man in Esqueda who rescued Clavel. He was still fidgeting with his fishing line, sitting in a chair.

I couldn't help but think of all the fish and other animals he'd killed in his long life. The enormous marlin and other sailfish hanging on the walls of his house, the rabbits, the foxes, and the doves he'd hunted; the pheasants, the elk, the shrimp, the octopus, the dorado, the grouper, the pigs, the sharks … and the countless deer like Clavel and his mother.

The list could go on and on, and he's only one man. I thought of all the hunters and fishermen in the world, and I thought of the global commercial fishing fleet—the destructive shrimp trawling, and the meat industry in general.

In light of the world around us, with its trail of death and destruction, one humble man, living in poverty in Esqueda, México, practicing kindness in the wilderness, is a miracle. Clavel is a miracle.

The authors of a study entitled *Biological Annihilation via the Ongoing Sixth Mass Extinction* describe the shrinking population of species as "a massive erosion of the greatest biological diversity in the history of Earth."

Some of the species already disappearing might not be widely known or have limited range, such as the Catarina pupfish, which is a tiny fish here in México now gone forever. It's not just Stan; it's all of us.

Gerardo Ceballos, an ecology professor at the Universidad Nacional Autónoma de México stated, "The massive loss of populations and species reflects our lack of empathy to all the wild species that have been our companions since our origins."

My father, an empathetic animal lover, but to whom the rules did not apply, accepted the man in México's inquiry to help Clavel the deer. He decided to fly the young deer back to the United States in our airplane with us. It seemed as though my father's own compassion was far larger than the small airplane he rode in on. The Mexican man and my father's mutual compassion combined for an illegal immigrant journey for a better future. USA, here we come!

So, how do you transport a 40-pound deer in an airplane cabin with other people? Duct tape and Nitrous Oxide—also known as *laughing gas,* the kind that dentists use.

Flying a deer across an international border in a four-seat aircraft with other humans on board is like putting a bottle of tequila on a candle lit table late a night, and then someone shouts, "Great idea!"

It just so happens that flying under the radar to avoid inquisitive US customs agents because of a wiggling deer can be challenging. It was a long flight. The anesthesia was wearing off. And I'm not sure they teach that kind of flying in flight training school. Ultimately, the results proved successful; our back yard became Clavel's new home.

Having Clavel was like living on a movie set. The neighbors' yards seemed dull, like cookie-cutter versions of run-of-the-mill suburbia in comparison.

Although traumatized early in life by hunters, duct tape, and Nitrous Oxide, Clavel's early adolescent life at our house was characterized by fun, love, and safety. We fed and cared for him. We also included him in our backyard games of adventure. We had a tree house, the woods, forts, and now it was transformed with an actual deer in it. Clavel was mostly shy, very gentle, and elegantly beautiful—living up to the qualities of his name, which means "carnation" in Spanish.

But all of that came to an end on the first day of rutting season. Rutting is when young deer get their antlers and rub their antlers against anything available. Clavel was bucking around in play more than normal. I noticed him acting differently this one morning. Bothered. Less docile. So, I suggested to my younger brother Jim to "go in there and see what's going on." I know, I know. This wasn't one of my best big-brother ideas. A deer rubbing his antlers against a tree is harmless enough. But it's a different story to watch a deer rub his antlers against the legs and back of an unsuspecting five-year-old kid.

Fortunately, Jim is quick, agile, and thinks fast on his feet—which served him well that day. Truly, I never imagined Clavel's unusually frisky behavior would result in him acting more like a bull than the passive and gentle deer that we knew. Jim's wild-eyed expression exiting the yard cast a world of displeasure in my direction for sending him in there in the first place.

With rutting season came the reality that Clavel needed to be free in the wild, for his sake as well as for ours. He was growing, and we knew it was time.

In spite of being raised by humans, he still retained most of his wild instincts, which my brother could attest to. So, we removed the red bandana and made arrangements to have him released into the San Gabriel Mountain wilderness. Unlike his last relocation, this move provided transportation that did not include duct tape and laughing gas.

The day Clavel left was a sad one for us, but I'm sure a very happy day for him. There was open space in the mountains, and a small population of other mule deer. We already knew Clavel could forage, since he ate almost everything in our yard.

I can relate to the vulnerable way in which Clavel's life began. We all have wounds. We should all be so lucky to experience the healing kindness of others. Being true to my own kindheartedness has been a life-long journey.

I remember what Clavel meant to me, and how much I loved him. I remember what he meant to my mother and father. And I can also imagine what Clavel must have meant to a kind, empathetic man in México who, with few resources, saved his life. I remember the improbability of it all. I remember Clavel's red bandana.

On the shores of the Sea of Cortez, Stan wiped his brow with his red bandana. An osprey was working the outer shore with dips and loops toward the ocean and sky. The sun was now warm and bright. A north wind line was capping about two miles offshore. Soon, a torrent of tumbling white wind waves will make it impractical for Stan to continue fishing.

Feebly, he cast his fishing line out to sea. The cast landed four feet out in the water from where he stood on shore and he nearly toppled over doing it. I was relieved he didn't fall face-first into the water requiring assistance. I also figured that with such a near-shore cast, there was no chance of hooking a fish. Good.

Just then, his fishing line pulled out to sea as he started to wrestle in a reddish brown snapper fish. Goddammit. Talk about pure luck! That cast he threw was a measly four feet out into the water!

The red snapper struggled for his life against the barbed hook and line pulling at its head.

And then with no particular urgency...as the snapper was suffocating in the air with a metal hook skewed into his mouth, Stan leisurely held the line up, shuffled back to his chair, sat down, stood up, searched for his rusty pair of pliers, shuffled around some more, dilly dallied, and then yanked the hook out of the fish's mouth. The poor fish tumbled to the ground, bouncing off the sand. The extreme stink-eye I threw out to Stan was laced with a profanity tirade in Spanish under my breath. *Mierda!—hijo de perra! Shit!—Son of a bitch!* These were a few of the words Lupita didn't teach me when I was a kid.

Ecologist and author Carl Safina told us what we already knew. Fish feel. He described fish sentience with scientific and anecdotal evidence. "Nerves, brain structure, brain chemistry and behavior—all evidence indicates that, to varying degrees, fish can feel pain, fear, and psychological stress. Research has also shown that various fish show long-term memory, social bonding, parenting, learned traditions, tool use, and even inter-species cooperation. Compared to those, pain and fear are primitive and basic."

Stan started to kick at the fish. He tried to kick the defenseless fish back toward the ocean, and I'd had about all I could take. Evidently, Stan's version of catch and release is to kick the fish back to the water.

Catch and release for Stan is a rarity. He's usually hauling in every last form of life from the ocean he can; snapper, eels, cabrera, squid, seahorses, starfish, anything and everything. He is a one-man shrimp-trawling boat; total destruction. The red snapper at Stan's feet was barely alive. She was traumatized and still suffocating, and Stan's big idea was to kick her back to the ocean? The cruelty of it ricochets in my heart even today.

Stan kicked at her again. The absurd scene was worlds apart from the comforting story fishermen like to tell themselves. The narrative goes something like this:

A big fish from another time waits for a worthy fishermen to free their restless spirit from the angry Sea and whoever catches that mystical beast of a fish will carry the spirit of the Ocean inside of them forever.

The harsh reality is a far cry from their romanticized version.

I leapt off the rock wall and ran down to save the helpless
fish and return her back to her home. My instincts kicked
in. I wanted to give her life back, or at least to give her
some dignity. Again, Stan balanced himself to take another
boot at her, causing me to further fume. I was tired of these
old men prowling the sanctuaries of our world torturing our
living, breathing earthlings while we sit on shore watching.

"I got it, Stan," I hollered, running over. "Hey! I got it!"

Surprised, Stan said, "Oh, I didn't think I was going to
catch anything today."

Yeah, no shit, I thought to myself. Gently but urgently, I
reached down and scooped up the fish. She gave another
desperate, possibly conclusive thrash for life. I put her in
knee-deep water and moved my hands with her trying to
revive her. She gasped again, trying to pull oxygen-rich
ocean water into her gills, and for several moments she
twisted side to side, sinking a little, and finally, crookedly
swam off. The harsh, cruel world rubbed up against the
wondrous Sea of Cortez.

I was too upset to say anything, so I sat silently with a distressed heart. I walked back to the seawall without making eye contact with Stan. I wanted so badly to unleash my most severe possible stink-eye, but didn't. I couldn't imagine why he wouldn't just lean over and pick the fish up and place her back in the ocean.

At moments like these, my mind would go inward and touch all directions. North, South, East, and West. My emotional compass was spinning. I'd lost my center, just as we as a species had lost our collective center.

I thought to myself, eight billion humans on Earth, with our hooks, and our guns, and our knives, and our boats, and our nets, and our boots…and our Stans of the world, kicking the fish. Nature didn't seem to have a chance.

I stood up atop the seawall, facing the ocean, deep into my own mind. With arms folded, I breathed in as if I was the precious little fish trying to inhale life back into my own body. Stan's son Marty, who must have seen the commotion, came out of the house and walked over to me.

Shoulder to shoulder, looking at the ocean he asked, "Is Dad ok?"

I glanced at Marty, utterly confused by the question, and then looked out at Stan. No mention of the fish pulled from her home, the fall she took landing on the sand, the kicking, the suffocating. The question is, "Is Dad ok?"

Flaccidly, I answered, "Yep, Stan's fine. But I'm not sure about the fish he caught. Stan was trying to kick her back into the ocean."

"Hmm… well, Stan doesn't know how to swim. Never did. I guess he was afraid of bending over and falling into the water," he replied.

Oh shit. I had no idea. It was easier to view Stan as an evil despotic type—a Captain Ahab—a crotchety old fool.

To paraphrase Nietzsche: *When fighting monsters, one should be careful not to become one.* Now look at me! Now I am the angry monster. I'm Captain Ahab.

My heart melted a little and my stink-eye softened. I thought of Lupita's son who didn't know how to swim and died from drowning in a river. I thought of Stan, that son of a bitch, and how many years he must have sat in boats while fishing, afraid to fall overboard. The ocean was not his friend. The ocean was his adversary.

I've spent more than 53 years knowing how to swim, and all this time with the ocean as my friend, my safe place, and the fishes my family. I hardly know what it's like otherwise.

It helped me to know about Stan's history—his not knowing how to swim. To see him from his son Marty's point of view, a fragile old man afraid of drowning. I was startled by how fast, with the help of my scathing eyes, I became what I hate—an uncaring, angry man.

Rustling my newfound empathy into action, like a scolded child I walked back down to the water's edge to present a question to Stan. "Let me help you pack up some of your stuff and I'll make a cup of coffee for ya. Whaddaya say?"

I was hoping to accomplish two things at once: to be kind and to end this dreadful fishing expedition of his. I focused my attention on the red bandana around his neck, trying to conjure up my memories of goodness and compassion.

Stan, oblivious to all of the daggers my eyes had been hurtling his way said, "Sure. I think I'm about done here."

Finally! I thought to myself, holding in any celebratory expressions.

I grabbed his chair to carry it up to the seawall, leaving him responsible for the fishing pole and tackle box. It's a slow walk off the sandy beach for the old man and me. His body, at 92 years old, is frail and uncertain. I set his chair down for him under the shade of a palapa by the seawall and told him I'd be right back with a couple of cups of coffee for us.

"Stan," I said. "Your red bandana reminds me of something. I remember it like it was yesterday …"

My plan? To share the unlikely, true story of how a humble man living in poverty in Esqueda, México met my father, and through their kindness, they rescued a deer named Clavel who wore a red bandana around his neck.

Chapter 7

THE DIRECTION OF TRUTH

The ocean has always been a powerful teacher for me. I've felt the softness of her touch. And I have been pummeled by fierceness of her strength. I've been held down deep underwater by a freight train of large waves for so long that my only remaining wish was for a tiny sip of precious air. I've seen the edge. I've been overpowered, humbled, reminded that I'm alive.

Her waves continue to teach me how to let go and when to relax. She teaches me when to move and when to stay still. She teaches me how to survive in a chaotic world by loosening my grip.

Don Quixote had windmills; I have waves. I've gracefully surfed waves as large as three story buildings—the famous, heavy waves of Maverick's—foggy-Humboldt-monster waves—and Mexican hurricane swell with no other Don Quixotes like me in the water.

I've spent sleepless nights listening to the lonely thunder of her waves pounding the dark night, penetrating my dreams, knowing the next morning I'll place myself in her powerful presence. She has held me in her peril. She has held me in her grace.

I've felt the release of her energy and escaped the latch of her grasp.

She is my teacher.

I am her student.

I'm endlessly mesmerized by her vitality. I see her wonder—her timeless dance with the moon. How her touch touches the breath of the wind, the pulsating tides and the skyscraper clouds that drench her, and us, with fresh water. I am captivated by how and when her waves break, the angle at which they arrive, the wash of foam as they explode. Sometimes, cloudy plumes of sand have been pulled into the wave from below. The cross chop from water ricocheting off rocks gives testament to her might. The number of waves in a set of waves, and the length of interval between them give her symmetry. The reef pulls and bends a wave like a branch bowing under the weight of heavy snow. Gremlin winds menace her surface. The infinite horizon provides so much to me, so much to all of us. I am a student of her waves like a shaman studies the inside of a mind.

She has taught me that I am small, temporary. In her giving she has taught me how to give, and how to be quiet.

Today, I am stoked—surfer jargon for happy. The euphoric buzz from surfing can last a brief time, or a lifetime.

"Monuments" is a left break, unusual for Baja. Left breaks are where the wave curls from right to left as it's surfed. It's the closest wave to Cabo San Lucas, so it can be crowded and sometimes unfriendly. I was nourished by the overhead fading south swell and the easygoing vibe of a rare wave-sharing morning at a fairly popular rocky point break. The abundance of waves from this particular swell, even though short, provided the opportunity for all the surfers to take turns sharing waves.

Sometimes, even aggressive surfers can't help themselves when it's that good. They too find themselves softened by the sculpting waters of the ocean. Her constant, generous, unprejudiced waves can transform us—meeting each of us where we are, not where we could be, or where we should be.

As I leave the ocean, I can still taste her salty kiss—drip-drying in delight. Sand is still stuck between my toes. Walking on land, the energy of her waves still under foot. On occasion, on my way home from a morning surf, I'll stop by my friend Mila's hip, farm-to-table style café located in the older section of the growing Mexican town of San José Del Cabo for a green juice and homemade tofu burger.

She didn't waste a second. "Oh hey, John!... I was just telling Marco, the easiest way to do it, ya know, by offering their lives, is to speak in a soft voice reverently, thank them, place them on the chopping block, and cut their throats." She said, "The chickens then need to hang headless, upside down, to drain the blood from their bodies...humane slaughter—I can teach you if you want."

She laughed at herself, amused, obviously trying to get a rise out of me. It certainly was abrupt enough to get my attention. But for the moment, her likely objective has the opposite effect on me. I go quiet. Mila doesn't always bombard me with graphic details of animal slaughter, but for some reason, today she was trying to get under my skin.

The glee in her voice as she theatrically explained the way the animals are "lovingly processed" combined with her effort to antagonize me makes me feel a little sad, like I'm an outsider, a freak—just because I prioritize compassion, I care, and I'm vegan. But I was far too mellow from surfing to play this game today.

Mila and I have an understanding. We share a mutual opposition to factory farming. We've even worked together at events to help educate the community and society in general about the destructive practices of land-based, industrial animal agriculture, and industrial fishing practices.

The global industrial fishing catch is over 100 million tons per year—so many fish that the official unit of measurement is weighed in tons instead of counting the billions of individual fish caught. One-half of all fish caught in the world's oceans are ground up for animal feed as a part of land-based factory farming. Roughly 45 million tons of ocean life is ground up as fishmeal and fed to pigs, chickens, and other land animals confined in large Concentrated Animal Feeding Operations (CAFOs).

The disconnection of destroying our precious ocean life in order to confine and slaughter animals on land is madness at it highest level. Mila opposes this as much as I do. We are allies on that front.

I let her descriptions of the so-called humane slaughtering operation and her antagonism go without response. *En boca cerrada no entran moscas – No flies enter a closed mouth.*

We've already had heated conversations about this topic, several in fact. I felt the inherent sadness of her dissonance, but the surf stoke—the love from the ocean I was feeling from my morning surf—helped me recognize the ineffectiveness of challenging her chosen worldview in that particular moment.

The words "humane" and "slaughter" don't seem to fit together, do they? Humane: showing compassion, or benevolence. Slaughter: to kill, butcher.

If I had used this kind of word combo in college, I might have heard my English professor say something like, "John, that is an awfully good example of a duplicitous and confusing oxymoron—and when we use an oxymoron without a poetic or ironic intention, it becomes a way to dull our intelligence."

As I mentioned, I was feeling generous. The ocean's loving, permissive surf vibe often helps quiet my sometimes-preachy self. So, for the moment, I duck-dived under a confrontational exchange with Mila about the deceptive humane slaughter label.

Later that day, arriving home, I read an *LA Times* article, describing violence in Baja, where bodies were found in San Jose Del Cabo in the early morning hours—victims of drug-related gang violence. It's horrible and upsetting that people capable of such harm live among us.

Perhaps I even knew the victims.

I had driven right past the aftermath on my way to surf that morning, without knowing the reality of the scene. A couple of police vehicles were present, but the normalcy of passersby gave the impression of the movie *Pleasantville*, not *Narcos-México.*

No lookie-loos. No hand-over-the-mouth stares. Nothing to see here, it seemed. This tourist town has a million-dollar industry to protect, and a narco-violent narrative would slow the stream of *gringo* tourists.

Surfers traveling into México have always been aware of the risks: theft, crooked cops, poor sanitation, and the problems of not letting the locals get the best waves. But most of the gringos like myself—and ex-pats—feel safer here in México than in the United States.

The friendly Mexican culture with its slower pace of life gives the impression of a less aggressive society with less violence. México's beauty is overwhelming and the American media has vastly overdramatized the dangers. But if you're running with the wrong crowd in México, the violence does exist.

The business of drug violence in México is brutal, and oftentimes swept under the rug. Many citizens are used to it, indifferent to it, and accept it as a fact of life. And the Mexican government and tourist associations tell the public that everything is fine.

Animal agriculture also has a shadow self. Poke, prod, cut, take, torture, kill, and hang all forms of animals, then put a happy face on it, tie a red bow on top, and tell people it's good for them.

I'm not equating animal agriculture to the drug cartel. But I can't help but notice the parallels. What I am saying is that our indifference to, or acceptance of, violence in all its forms has created the world we live in.

I simply want us to be honest about what we see. As Clarissa Pinkola Estes wrote, *"Let us tie our shoes and walk in the direction of truth."*

After finishing my curry tofu burger with sweet potato fries at Mila's cafe, I spotted Mila and said, "Thank you..." with a slight hesitation.

"Annddd..." she says, exaggerating the moment.

I was edging around the opportunity to say something—again—about the misinformation regarding humane slaughter. I wanted to tell her that we must become people who look at things head-on. We mustn't weave dark, damning shrouds into fairy tales of celebration.

Just the other day, I went to a vigil at a slaughterhouse in La Paz, México. A group of six of us, mostly young women and I would ask the truck drivers bringing animals to the slaughterhouse for three minutes of their time to say goodbye to the cows and pigs being transported to their deaths. It was 99 degrees Fahrenheit with no shade. All the animals were completely distressed, suffering from heat exhaustion and fear. At times, the smells, and the heat, and anxiety of the animals overwhelmed us.

A six-month-old calf—a baby—was brought to the slaughterhouse because the owner couldn't afford to keep feeding her. She was so frightened she kept throwing herself against the bars of the truck, trying to leap out. A three-year-old pig with an open wound on his nose was so heat-distressed that when we squirted water into his mouth he couldn't swallow because he was panting so heavily.

I was so impressed and inspired by the girls and women in our group—some in their teens, some their twenties. Just like in the United States, the culture of México can be machismo, degrading to women, while treating the animals going to slaughter like objects.

We affirmed the life of the animals at the slaughterhouse gates and witnessed their suffering. Not everyone needs to bear witness to such suffering. But let us not call that nonsense "humane." It is not.

Mila persisted, "Is there something else you'd like to say?"

"Yes!" I said, accentuating the dramatic. "Thank you *very* much!" Again, I bit my tongue and kept my thoughts to myself.

She and I have already discussed the humane slaughter fairytale. The topic has been well covered between us.

I rarely miss an opportunity to speak my mind. That way, I'm able to flamboyantly declare the world a better place for having heard my thoughts. My wife Carol is a saint. Saint Carol. She's heard it all. Every single thought, every last opinion of mine has landed on her angelic ears. She nods—usually in agreement—says wise things, and then typically suggests that I write about it. So, I write down the bones, the sadness, the hope, the journals, the poems, the lectures, and the rants. Scribbling noises in my notebook silence a thousand crickets.

I have to admit it, keeping quiet sometimes feels heroic. To an ordinary person it probably feels normal. But to me, it feels like I've accomplished something extraordinary.

Being in the ocean mist of her waves on that crystal clear morning stayed with me. The patience I developed while waiting for waves. The water's vibration coated the inner workings of my mind. I thought again of water—humble, flexible, determined, and non-judgmental. The loving ocean meets me where I am, in the sometimes less than enlightened situation I find myself—me being me—passionate, arrogant, sometimes judgmental.

I too can meet Mila where she is, in the sometimes less than enlightened situation I find her—passionate, arrogant, sometimes judgmental.

The "Golden Rule" of doing unto others as we would want done unto us is the principle I wish Mila would consider for the animals she kills, or pays others to have killed for her restaurant. But I also need to consider the Golden Rule for my interactions with Mila. Would I want someone like me to continue to bring up the same topic of veganism day after day? Neither of us would have gained anything from another debate about humane slaughter.

I can't confront every animal-eating restaurant owner about their cognitive dissonance as if I am the lone voice of compassion for animals. There are many others who feel the same as I do. More and more people every day are choosing healthier plant-based foods that don't cause needless harm to animals.

My life is brief, as brief as the ephemeral light on a wave at sunrise. I need to use my time wisely, and also choose my words wisely. I am a voice for animals, and for the ocean. This won't change.

But sometimes being quiet is the biggest impact I can have. I've learned this too from my wife, Saint Carol. So, I write it all down. Deep in my notebook, a butterfly migrates to México. It is inescapable—to be steered to a higher self. This moment has prepared me for the next moment. My life is a remarkable thing. All of life is.

A few days later, on Christmas day, our neighbor Lupe and her niece, Rosa, made a vegan meal of chili rellenos, potato enchiladas, and rice and beans for our family. I asked if they had done anything special for the holidays. She said it was a busy time of year but the entire family made a *nacimiento*, or nativity scene, decorated with *flores secas*, dried flowers. The dried flowers, she explained, are to always keep the ideals of hope and peace alive.

I imagined the nativity—people and animals lovingly look toward a vulnerable, newborn child. A star shines brightly in the night sky in an atmosphere of kindness, safety, and peace.

I ended my day where it had begun, at the edge of the sea with my notebook and an evening cup of tea, sitting on the beach. Writing in this notebook, there is no deception. This is why I write. I write the truth about me. I pause and I look out at the Sea—in the direction of truth—searching for the right words. As if the right words about truth and dreaming of a better world exist. They don't.

I decided to be as truthful as possible. I picked up the pen but there was nothing to say or write. Mimicking the boundlessness and humility of the Sea itself, I left the notebook behind on the beach and chose instead to swim in her waters.

I'll find the right words later. Perhaps in the morning—I'll find them in the flotsam and jetsam along the tide lines of the shore.

Words made from driftwood and broken shells and battered pieces of tile—the consequences of our imperfect world.

Chapter 8

A TURTLE NEST

The tiniest pebble has a voice.

It was an overcast morning. We were walking south along
the shore with the sunrise in front of us.

If Carol and I hadn't seen the female Olive Ridley sea turtle
on the beach laboriously crawling back to the Sea of Cortez
in the morning light, we wouldn't have known that she
buried her eggs in the sand. The arduous trail she left from
the sea and then back again was very distinctive—a path
with two-winged shovel marks from her legs on the
opposites sides of what looks like a heavy bag dragged
through the sand.

She sows her expectant dream of life into the earth with
over one hundred eggs implanted for safekeeping. The nest

is a jerrybuilt shack in the sand, with comma-shaped clouds.

Some people follow the teachings of Jesus, Mohammad, or the Buddha. I follow the teachings of the ocean.

It is the beating heart of life—below the surface—hidden from view, or sometimes within view. It is the synthesis of a wave, or the essence buried in the sand under my feet, lying dormant.

As a surfer, I see a wave as a pulse of information containing the spontaneity of life, and the web of life ensnares my soul.

An ocean friend of mine, Dr. Sylvia Earle, puts it less esoterically: "No ocean, no life. No blue, no green. No ocean, no us."

Only two or three out of the hundreds of baby turtles who hatch will live to be ten years old. That"s the age when the turtles begin to reproduce. The baby turtles' natural predators include coyotes, feral dogs, **large crabs**, snakes, frigate birds, seagulls, fishes, and sharks.

And not surprisingly, the turtle's other most significant threat to living to maturity is humans. While illegal egg-poaching is not as rampant as it used to be—a sign that cultures can change—our fishing practices are a significant threat. Trawling nets, gill nets, ghost nets, long line fishing, and countless other forms of pillaging the ocean kill untold turtles, not to mention the vehicles driven on the beaches in México.

Tourists and locals alike have grown accustomed to using the beach as a playground for off-road vehicles, or simply as a road for casual transport into town. Look out—slow moving baby turtles crawling to the sea for the first time! Henry Ford, beep beep, coming through!

It is thought by many Buddhists that Padmasambhava, the 8th-century Indian saint who brought Buddhism to Tibet, also hid spiritual teachings called *termas* in caves, forests, lakes, and even in the sky to be found by realized adepts at particular times in history when they would be most needed.

He concealed these secret teachings in knowledge time capsules of sorts to later be fortuitously uncovered at just the right moment to help humanity.

I wondered if the buried sea turtle nests incubating on our beaches were trying to tell us something?

Roughly two million ocean animals are killed globally *every minute* in our industrial fishing operations.

Dr. Sylvia Earle also said, "The Ocean is the cornerstone of earth's life support system; it shapes climate and weather. It holds most of life on earth. Ninety-seven percent of earth's water is there. It's the blue heart of the planet—we should take care of our heart."

The ocean absorbs more carbon dioxide, and produces more oxygen, than all trees on land. Her waters breathe life into our world—so utterly valuable, yet unrecognized, and now in jeopardy.

Carol and I decided to protect the turtle nest by putting bamboo stakes in the sand around the area where, at sunrise, we saw the female turtle painstakingly pull her way back to the sea. Here, in southern Baja, México, the circular stakes seem to be understood as the universal symbol for turtle nest. For good measure, like protective parents we tied a sign around one of the bamboo posts written in both

English and Spanish announcing that this was indeed a turtle nest.

So, for 60 days, the eggs' gestation period, we talked to over 60 people, at least one person a day. Chatting with neighbors, passers by walking the beach, and my favorite folks: the ones riding the ATVs. All good conversations, no judgment, no lectures, just smiles; a happy exchange of turtle nest info—egg gestation length, types of turtle species in the area, and the damage fishing has on the ocean, as well as the damage riding motorized vehicles has on the beach.

Our own hearts—or as Tibetan Buddhists refer to it, our heart-minds—just may be our greatest treasure. Everyone we talked to revealed a sense of wonder and empathetic care for the vulnerable eggs in the sand. We are hardwired with the wisdom of compassion. It comes naturally, but the voice of wisdom seems so distant, buried so deep.

It wasn't all "Kumbaya" at the turtle nest. There was no made-for-Hollywood eureka moments. No, it was subtler than that.

What we did see was the lights begin to shine in people's

eyes. We saw that people felt sincere care for the turtle nest. We got a sense that their hearts opened, just a little.

As it turned out, the eggs in the nest of this particular Olive Ridley turtle never hatched. Not one. My friend Omar from the Grupo Tortueguero suggested that the air temperature could have been too cold this time of year for the eggs to incubate.

It may also have been a "false crawl." A false crawl is where a female turtle emerges from the water with the intention of laying a nest but was disturbed by conditions on the beach and returns to the ocean without laying her eggs. Simple disturbances like noise, people, lights, or objects on the beach can cause a false crawl. All of the familiar markings in the sand indicated to us it wasn't a false crawl and that eggs were laid, but perhaps not.

As far as I know, the sea turtle is the only ocean animal that leaves her home, the water, and travels onto land to have her babies.

The sea turtles seem to be saying: "These are my offspring, my future, all of life, as I know it. I place them at your feet, in the sand. Take good care of them. Take good care of this place, my nest. I'm entrusting this to you." Then, back into the ocean the female turtles swim.

Our response? Hop on the ATV, kids! We're going for a drive on the beach, and bring the fishing poles!

We'll never know for sure why these specific eggs from this particular nest didn't hatch. Perhaps the nest was damaged somehow when it was unattended. Or there is a health issue with her. Who knows?

What I do know is that humanity needs help. We're consuming many species into extinction. We don't value ocean conservation as much as we value making money, or eating animals, or recreating with ATV's on the beach.

I would like to believe that turtle nests could be the equivalent of a Buddhist terma, a buried teaching.

Ideas can awaken with seeming spontaneity, like an ocean wave arriving, seemingly out of the blue. But that single ocean wave that finally expended her energy on shore may have traveled across the surface of the ocean for weeks, across long distances. She is a pulse of energy, a capsule of information, the mix of wind and water that then becomes a wave.

Sometimes, when planting seeds of hope, the seeds come to fruition in a recognizable form, like baby turtles. Sometimes, the seeds we plant don't come to realization in the time and place we expect. We can't always see the results of our prayers, and our deepest desires.

Some say at birth, Padmasambhava manifested from a ray of light from the heart of the Buddha. So, in other words, he was so enlightened he was born inside the very essence of enlightenment itself. His spiritual teachings are awaiting us to uncover them, encouraging us to awaken.

On the other side of the coin; my mother would have been happy if I had just stopped poking myself in the eye on the day I was born. I am imperfect, like everyone else.

Because I see both myself and others as being far from Padmasambhava's ideals of enlightenment, I have a more realistic and doable vision for our world. Maybe a five percent shift of consciousness would be enough to turn things around for us with the oceans. Perhaps we could stop poking ourselves in the eye.

Marine Biologists describe how the next ten years for the ocean is likely to be the most important time in the next 10,000 years. And, that we have options that we're going to lose within ten years unless we take action. When an ocean species goes extinct, it's forever.

"No ocean, no life. No blue, no green. No ocean, no us."

After an evening yoga class, Carol and I joined the folks on the beach, near where the turtle laid her eggs, to watch the colors of sundown. From where we sat, a colony of seagulls already circled the moon above us. My wife's painted toenails stick out in the sand like shiny red pieces of sea glass.

We chatted about the beauty and mystery of how sea turtles navigate at sea by sensing the lines of Earth's magnetic field. This turtle navigation system is similar to the ancient Polynesian navigators' method of using stars, observation of birds, and the use of waves and swells, but all rolled up into one internal GPS system. Mother turtles will return year after year to the same beach to lay eggs, and those offspring will return to that very same beach to do the same.

I thought back to that evening's yoga class. As we laid resting in *Savassana*, the teacher had read a short poem by the Indian saint Saraha:

Though the house-lamps have been lit,
The blind live on in the dark.
Though spontaneity is all-encompassing and close,
To the deluded it remains
Always far away.

The high-water mark of broken shells was near us. We heard their voices, muffled in the sand. Aligned to the right frequency, my wife decided which language to use, while the waves exchanged colors with the sky. Fourteen seconds of silence between the rhythms of information.

Waiting for the turtles to return, we counted the waves one by one, like *milagros* from the Basilica of the Sea.

Chapter 9

TAKE ACTION

The Facts

- By 2048, every single marine ecosystem will have been destroyed from over-fishing. Some scientists say that may happen even sooner, factoring in ocean warming, and plastic pollution.

- As many as 2.7 trillion animals are pulled from the ocean in fishing nets and lines every single year.

- 3/4 of the world's fisheries are exploited or depleted.

- For every 1 pound of fish caught, up to 5 pounds of unintended marine species are caught and discarded as by-kill.

- Scientists estimate as many as 650,000 whales, dolphins and seals are killed every year by fishing vessels.

- 40-50 million sharks are killed in fishing lines and nets.

- More than 50 percent of the fish taken from the ocean is converted into animals feed for pigs, chickens, and cows.

- 70 billion farmed animals are reared annually worldwide. More than 6 million animals are killed for food every hour.

- Animal agriculture is responsible for 18 percent of greenhouse emissions, more than the combined exhaust from all transportation.

- Animal agriculture is responsible for 80-90% of all U.S. water consumption.

- Animal livestock covers 45% of Earth's total land.

- Animal agriculture is the leading cause of species

extinction, ocean dead zones, water pollution, and habitat destruction.

Adopting a vegan diet puts compassion and ocean conservation into action.

- A person who follows a vegan diet produces the equivalent of 50 percent less carbon dioxide, uses 1/11th oil, 1/13th water, and 1/18th land compared to a meat-lover for their food.

- Each day, a person who eats a vegan diet saves 1,100 gallons of water, 45 pounds of grain, 30 square feet of forested land, 20 pounds CO2 equivalent, and one animal's life.

Veganism is the most ecological positive lifestyle for humanity. I am vegan because I love the ocean and I love life.

Please consider adopting a vegan diet for the sake of your health, for the sake of the oceans, and for the sake of the animals.

ACKNOWLEDGMENTS

In Hawai'i, in the summer of 1974, my mother, Anne Merryfield insisted I keep a journal. With great resistance, as if using Twitter's 140-character limit, I scribbled notes about where I surfed each day and the ocean life I encountered. It is through my mother's love of language that I developed my own connection to writing. I am eternally grateful to her for her positivity and her continued inspiration.

Benjamin Allen's friendship and his deep understanding of my world of waves and water are beyond measure. The contributions of Jasmin Singer, Roberto Wright, and Deborah Brown were generous and instrumental.

My wife Carol is my poetry. She is my infinite ocean in a world of people.

ABOUT THE AUTHOR

John Merryfield is a poet, surfer, and co-author of the book, *Vegan 1 Day: Stories of Living the Good Life.* He has appeared on Outside TV, and Tahoe TV, and is also a contributor to the *Moonshine Ink, Sierra Sun, Simply Haiku* journal, *Notes from the Gean* journal, and the *Elephant* journal. He lives with his wife Carol in Kings Beach, California and Buenavista, Baja, México.